LAW
SCHOOL

A Survivor's Guide

LAW SCHOOL

A Survivor's Guide

- The Socratic Method
- The Faculty
- Moot Court
- Law Review
- Exams
- Finding a Job
- And Other Legal Stuff

JAMES D. GORDON III

ILLUSTRATIONS BY ROLLIN McGRAIL

HarperPerennial

A Division of HarperCollins*Publishers*

HarperCollins books may be purchased for educational, business, or sales promotional use. For information please write: Special Markets Department, HarperCollins Publishers, Inc., 10 East 53rd Street, New York, NY 10022.

FIRST EDITION

Designed by Irving Perkins Associates

Library of Congress Cataloging-in-Publication Data

Gordon, James D., 1954–
    Law school : a survivor's guide / James D. Gordon III. — 1st ed.
        p.   cm.
    Includes bibliographical references and index.
    ISBN 0-06-095055-2 (pbk.)
    1. Law schools—United States—Humor.   2. Lawyers—United States—
Humor.   I. Title.
K184.G67   1994
340'.071'173—dc20   92-56209

94   95   96   97   98   AC/RRD   10   9   8   7   6   5   4   3   2   1

To Nadine,
who loves a lawyer

Contents

Preface

This is supposed to be a funny book about law school, lawyers, and the law. As Abraham Lincoln said, "For those who like this kind of a book, this is the kind of a book they will like."

However, I have discovered that some people—mostly lawyers and people who have married, parented, or housebroken lawyers—are scandalized by the book. To those people, I sincerely extend my heartfelt understanding and genuine compassion. And I say, "Stuff a sock in it." Next to politicians (and there usually is a lawyer next to one), lawyers constitute perhaps the most powerful and wealthy elite in our society. They are well educated, articulate, and completely able to defend themselves. If we can't make fun of lawyers, who can we make fun of? (This is a rhetorical question. The answer it suggests, of course, is "Politicians." But before you think of that, I'll move on.)

In large measure, ours is a society run by lawyers. They write our laws, interpret our laws, enforce our laws, and defend those who break our laws. They have considerable power to decide the direction of our society. If we satirize our society—and I submit that it deserves it—lawyers should be one of the biggest targets. Humor is a weapon available to everyone. It's cheaper than rocket launchers, and it doesn't kill innocent civilians (which pleases Democrats) or destroy property (which pleases Republicans). It permits the slaughtering of a few sacred cows without getting up to your ankles in red goopy stuff (which pleases the Board of Health, as well as your dry cleaner). So I suggest to the stuffed-shirted scandalized: lighten up. Meanwhile, I am exploring my options in the federal witness-protection program.

Over the years I have collected stories, witticisms, half-witticisms, and nit-witticisms from many people. I owe thanks (and some apologies) to Jae Ballif, Steve Barton, Vern Baugh, Dee Benson, Gertrude Block, Juanita Brooks, Jan Harold Brunvand, Eliot Butler, Linda Bytoff, Patrick Cathcart, Steven Chidester, Jesse Choper, Mike Cohen, Jack Coons, Ron Degnan, Mike DeGroote, Paul Duke, Vaughn J. Featherstone, Cliff Fleming, Frank Fox, Barney Frank, Fred Gedicks, Mike Goldsmith, Doug Gordon, Craig Griffin, Bob Gulack, Bruce Hafen, Jon Hafen, Arne Hallam, Carl Hawkins, Kenney Hegland, Duane Hiatt, Martin Hickman, Samuel Hoffenstein, Junius Hoffman, Jeffrey R. Holland, Paul Hughes, Greg Husisian, Gene Jacobs, Bob Johnson, Ed Kimball, Carmen Kipp, Rex Lee, Virginia Lim, Neil Lindberg, Hans Linde, Constance Lurdberg, Jay Lunt, Mike McConnell, Steve Nelson, Eric Nielson, Dallin H. Oaks, Doug Parker, Tom Read, Janet Robinson, Dan Rodriguez, Leslie Rosenthal, Bob Sackett, John Sansing, DeWitt Scott, Bud Scruggs, Dick Selfridge, Alison Selfridge, Marjorie Shultz, Barry Silverman, Steve Smith, Mark Stoddard, Tim Stratford, John Tanner, Toby Threet, Mark Van Wagoner, Jan Vetter, J. Clifford Wallace, Paul Warner, Dale Whitman, Kevin Worthen, Tim Zinnecker, Claude Zobell, and others. I am also grateful for the comments and suggestions of Scott Cameron, Dave Chipman, Tony D'Amato, Ray Davis, Mike Goldsmith, Bob Gulack, Kenney Hegland, Greg Husisian, Gene Jacobs, Marianne Jennings, Erik Jensen, Ed Kimball, Alex Kozinski, and Val Ricks, and for the research assistance of Dave Coleman, Gary Hill, Bruce Murdock, and Kory Staheli. Special thanks go to my editor, Cynthia Barrett, production editor Dot Gannon, and assistant editor Ari Hoogenboom. Many thanks also to my agents, Gail Ross and Leslie Breed. Still others have insisted, while fingering sharp objects, that they would prefer not to have their names mentioned anywhere in this book.

Portions of this book have previously appeared in *How Not to Succeed in Law School*, reprinted by permission of The Yale Law Journal Company and Fred B. Rothman & Company from *The Yale Law Journal*, Vol. 100, pp. 1679–1706 (1991); *Oh No! A New Bluebook!*, 90 Mich. L. Rev. 1698 (1992); *The Trials of Reforming Legal Education*, Chron. Higher Ed., Jan. 22, 1992, at B1; *Law*

Review and the Modern Mind, 33 Ariz. L. Rev. 265 (1991); *An Unofficial Guide to the Bill of Rights*, 1992 B.Y.U. L. Rev. 371; and A *Bibliography of Humor and the Law*, 1992 B.Y.U. L. Rev. 427.

Well, that's enough of a Preface. Let's get to the text and start the statute of limitations running on the libel suits.

CHAPTER

1

Should You Go to
Law School?

Would you like to help the less fortunate?

Would you like to see liberty and justice for all?

Do you want to vindicate the rights of the oppressed?

If so, you should join the Peace Corps. The last thing you should do is attend law school.

People basically hate lawyers, and with good reason. That's why you'll rarely escape from a dinner party without hearing at least one lawyer joke. For example:

QUESTION: You're walking down the beach and you come upon Saddam Hussein and a lawyer buried up to their necks in sand. Who do you kick first?

ANSWER: Saddam Hussein. Business before pleasure.

FIRST CHILD: My dad is a lawyer.

SECOND CHILD: Honest?

FIRST CHILD: No, he's just like the rest of them.

A terrorist group kidnapped one hundred lawyers. They threatened that unless their demands were met they would release them one at a time.

1

*   *   *

Recently there was a classified ad in the *National Review* that said: "Hate Lawyers? Curse out a live one. 900/773–8245. $5/min. 18 or older."[1]

Literature reveals that people have ALWAYS hated lawyers. Samuel Coleridge wrote, in *The Devil's Thoughts:*

> He saw a Lawyer killing a Viper
> On a dunghill hard by his own stable;
> And the Devil smiled, for it put him in mind
> Of Cain and his brother Abel.[2]

So the public hates lawyers. Of course, what does the public know? Studies show that one-third of the public suffers from some kind of severe mental disorder. So look at the people on each side of you. If they look normal to you, then you're the one.[3]

However, even other species detest lawyers. Carl Sandburg wrote:

> Why is there always a secret singing
> When a lawyer cashes in?
> Why does a hearse horse snicker
> Hauling a lawyer away?[4]

But this animal animosity is not justified. It's true that some lawyers are dishonest, arrogant, greedy, venal, amoral, ruthless buckets of toxic slime. On the other hand, it is unfair to judge the ENTIRE profession by five or six hundred thousand bad apples.

In fact, there are many perfectly legitimate reasons for going to law school. For example, ask yourself the following questions:

---

[1] [*So Noted*], Cal. Law. Apr. 1992, at 19.

[2] Samuel Coleridge, *The Devil's Thoughts*, in *Complete Poetical Works* 320 (1912).

[3] Question: How many psychiatrists does it take to change a light bulb?
Answer: Only one, but the light bulb has to want to change.

[4] Carl Sandburg, *The Lawyers Know Too Much*, in *Complete Poems* 189 (1950).

Do I want to go to medical school but can't stand the sight of blood?

Are my inlaws pestering me to death to do something meaningful (*i.e.*, lucrative) with my life? Have I considered circulating petitions to ban inlaws, but realized that it would only spawn stupid bumper stickers saying, "WHEN INLAWS ARE OUTLAWED, ONLY OUTLAWS WILL HAVE INLAWS"?

Did I major in English and have absolutely nowhere else to turn?

Did I grow up watching *Perry Mason* reruns? I used to watch *Perry Mason*, but the ending was always predictable. Mason would be brilliantly cross-examining a witness, and somebody in the courtroom would jump up and blurt out that he or she was actually the guilty party. I could never figure out why the murderers always attended the trial. Why weren't they halfway to Rio de Janeiro?

The long-running *Perry Mason* series left a generation of Americans believing that most criminal defendants are innocent, that district attorneys are whining incompetents, and that lawyers and private investigators have shoulders as large as sides of beef.[5] It

---

[5] Perry Mason's wardrobe was later purchased by Jay Leno.

also left them believing that lawyering is an exciting lifestyle, since Mason never sat through endless depositions, answered interrogatories, supervised document productions, or even spent much time at his desk. Fortunately, these misconceptions were corrected by the *cinéma vérité* of *L.A. Law.*

Anyway, for one reason or another, you might begin to feel that law school is for you. If so, as Mark Twain said, lie down for a while until the feeling goes away. If it doesn't go away, prepare yourself for the consequences.

For instance, your grandparents will immediately scrape off their bumper sticker that says, "ASK ME ABOUT MY GRANDCHILDREN." You see, they grew up in a time when a person's word was his bond, when a handshake was enough, when disputes were worked out amicably and quickly among people of goodwill. Fortunately, *you* don't live in such primitive times! Today, you can make a handsome income exploiting other people's personal tragedies and society's declining sense of community. And just in time, too—just as you are graduating from college. Talk about lucky!

Taking the LSAT

Before you can go to law school, you have to take an exam called the LSAT. Nobody knows whether the "A" in LSAT stands for "Admissions," "Aptitude," or "Arbitrary." The LSAT basically measures how well you can use a Number 2 pencil to fill in the little circles on the computer sheet. Be sure to fill in the circles completely and carefully. Do not make any stray marks on the paper. This will lower your score. The instructions at the top of the exam carefully explain that these are the grading criteria, but hardly anyone ever pays any attention to them. Most people think that the exams are graded according to the correctness of the answers. HA!

The LSAT scoring system used to go up to 800, but recently the LSAT people (whoever they are) changed it so that now the highest possible score is 180. This looks pretty suspicious, if you ask me. I mean, why 180? Why not a nice round number, like 100? The secret truth is that a group of law professors who scored 180 on the old exam lobbied the LSAT people to make 180 the highest score. The LSAT people cheerfully complied, once it was made clear to them that law schools did not have to use the LSAT anymore at all. They could use the same approach used by most graduate schools: random selection.

The old LSAT had—I am not kidding—a math section. But

the LSAT people finally realized that no one had asked a lawyer to solve a quadratic equation or find the cosine of an angle for, probably, several centuries, and so they eventually deleted it. This action was taken against their better judgment (using the term loosely). After all, the math section provided a handy way to discriminate among people of equal intelligence.

Frankly, the new LSAT isn't much better. It asks questions like, "Compare Madam Defarge in *A Tale of Two Cities* with Huckleberry Finn in *Huckleberry Finn*." This makes no sense at all, as lawyers hardly ever have to address this question.

Another question is:

> Assume you have a fox, a goose, and a bag of corn. You need to row them all across the river, but the boat will carry only you and one other thing at a time. If you leave the fox and the goose alone, the fox will eat the goose. If you leave the goose and the corn alone, the goose will eat the corn. How do you get them across?

The answer is so simple a child could get it: you beat the goose unconscious with an oar, and then take the fox across before he flees for his life. This question is so stupid I don't even know why they include it.

It never seems to have occurred to the LSAT people that their test might deign to include a few questions that actually relate to a lawyer's work. For example:

1. The judge receives a bribe of $5,000 from the plaintiff's lawyer. He then receives a bribe of $10,000 from the defendant's lawyer. The judge should:
   A. Notify the state bar association.
   B. Notify the police.
   C. Notify the FBI.
   D. [The correct answer.] Return $5,000 to the defendant and try the case on its merits.

2. Mark is an honest lawyer who learns that his client is guilty of a heinous crime. Mark should:

A. Tell the judge.
B. Tell the police.
C. Withdraw from the representation.
D. Defend his client but not argue that his client is innocent.

Answer: This is a trick question. There is no such thing as an honest lawyer.

The LSAT people say that LSAT preparation courses do not help, since the LSAT tests knowledge and skills that cannot be improved by last-minute cramming. Regardless of what the LSAT people say, however, you will notice that there are several suspiciously solvent LSAT prep course companies who are happy to take your money anyway. Of course, you can always choose to "go bare" and take the LSAT without any prep course at all. People who have done this in the past are called "nonlawyers."

You take the LSAT in a stifling room crammed with 500 sweating people who have apparently never watched a deodorant commercial in their entire life. Through a strange quirk of fate, you have to sit right next to some moron who chomps loudly on corn nuts throughout the whole exam while wearing those artillery-range ear protectors that make it impossible for him to notice anything less than 7.5 on the Richter Scale. They also make it impossible for you to tell him what an inconsiderate imbecile he is. Notice your feeling of panic and nausea as you take the LSAT. Get used to it.

After you take the LSAT, they send you your score and a statement explaining which "percentile" you are in. The "percentile" is the inverse percentage chance you have of spending your life doing something honest.

CHAPTER 3

Applying to Law School

Now that you have received your LSAT score, you have to decide which law schools to apply to. The official motto of law schools is: "Turning America into lawyers, one human being at a time." There are many fine law schools to choose from. For instance:

Boalt Hall (Berserkeley). Boalt is built on a hill overlooking one of the most spectacular views on earth: the San Francisco Bay and the Golden Gate Bridge. Therefore, the building was designed with lots of huge picture windows. Then, inexplicably, they ROTATED the building ninety degrees so that all its picture windows face directly into the fraternity houses across the street. You can't catch a glimpse of the bay, but you do have a terrific view of fraternity blobs sitting around in their gym shorts, drinking beer, belching, and listening to the music of Metallica at 300 decibels.

The puny little side doors became the front doors, and in order to make the side doors look like front doors, school officials placed quotes by famous Supreme Court justices above the doors—like "Go forth and practice law like blazes." This quote sounds pretty stupid now, but at the time it was considered one of the wisest things a Supreme Court justice had ever said.

Case Western Reserve. A combination law school and game preserve. *Cf.* Wake Forest.

Chicago. Learn how many Chicago law professors it takes to screw in a light bulb. (Answer: None. The market will take care of it itself.)

Columbia. On the front of the law school building at Columbia, you will notice a huge sculpture of a man who has put a noose around the neck of a horse and is throttling it to death. You will not be able to understand the true significance of this sculpture until several days into your first year at Columbia.

George Mason. Founded by Perry's younger brother, George. George Mason emphasizes law and economics, thus increasing the supply of lawyer economists. Now all they need is a demand curve.

Harvard. Harvard is number one, as you can learn by asking anyone who went to Harvard. Or even if you don't ask. The only disadvantage of going to Harvard is that the graduation robes are the same color as Balls o' Fire Salmon Eggs.

Iowa. The law school is shaped like a circle. This makes perfect sense, since most law professors talk in them anyway. Iowa has a large law library, with a square footage of $r^2 (\alpha - \sin \alpha)/2$.

Louisiana State. Study Louisiana law, ninety-five percent of which deals with how to draw boundary lines in swamp water.

Michigan. This is a good school, except that when winter is over someone will have to remind you not to stare at that big yellow ball in the sky. If you trip over something as you walk to class in January, it might be the top of a telephone pole sticking out of the snow.

New York University. NYU charges the highest tuition, on the theory—called the Ray-Ban theory—that people will note the price tag and conclude that it must be the best school. Or maybe it's because everything costs a fortune in New York. Just buying a newspaper will exceed the credit limit on your Master-Card.

Northwestern. This school is *not* located in the Northwest, but in Chicago. However, the founders thought that "Midwest-

ern" sounded kind of hokey. Northwestern should not be confused with Lewis and Clark Northwestern, which really *is* in the Northwest, or with Northeastern, Southwestern, or Southern. Bring a mariner's compass to keep them straight. Northwestern's goal is that eventually people will refer to Harvard as "the Northwestern of the Northeast."

Pennsylvania. Located in a city founded on the principles of peace, love, tolerance, and parading around in chicken feathers once a year. Lawyers can meet at least one of these requirements.

St. John's, St. Louis, St. Mary's, St. Thomas, San Diego, San Francisco, and **Santa Clara.** Saintly law schools. Have you ever noticed that few lawyers have been canonized? Many lawyers, however, have been cannonized.

Stetson. Mad Hatter School of Law.

Virginia. Widely known in Charlottesville as "the Harvard of Charlottesville."

Wayne State University. For people who want to practice law in the State of Wayne. Located in stately Wayne Manor.

Yale. Forget about Yale. It's so selective that *no one* ever goes there. Ask yourself this: Do you personally know anyone who is going there *now?* Of course not. Oh, sure, there are lots of people who say that they went there in the PAST, now that it can't be verified. Don't *you* be fooled.

Law schools can be divided into three categories:

1. The Top Ten. There are about twenty-five schools in this category. Consult this week's AP and CNN polls.
2. The "Middle Group," which includes all other accredited law schools. These schools actually teach the law.
3. About 2,000 unaccredited California law schools, like Frank and Morty's School of Law and Cosmetology of the Lower Level of the Seven Hills Shopping Mall. Don't let the classy name fool you. There are basically two requirements for admission:

1. A pulse.
2. $12,000.

The first requirement can be waived.

Also, be sure to avoid law schools with "Jr." in the name, like "Leland Stanford Jr. Law School." These are actually junior law schools.

People often ask whether they should attend a law school in the state where they intend to practice. The answer is NO. A good law school's curriculum is not tied to the law of any particular state. This is also true of the "elite" law schools, except that their curriculum is not tied to the law of any particular planet. You should attend one of those schools if you intend to practice law somewhere in the Andromeda galaxy.

You will need to submit applications to several law schools, which will cost you fifty bucks a pop. Law schools have you fill out lengthy application forms which require you not only to provide your GPA and your LSAT score, but also to describe your unique abilities and experiences and ways in which you might add to the rich fabric of the law school class. It takes you about eighty hours apiece to fill out these forms. It takes you even more time to write and polish and repolish the "personal statement." Check over your personal statement carefully to make certain that you have used the two key words every law school looks for: "endeavor" and "cognitive." If all else fails, slip in a sentence such as "I have always endeavored to be cognitive in all my cognitive endeavors."

When the law school receives your application, it banks your check, adds up your GPA and your LSAT, and throws the rest of the application away. I mean, if you were one of only two employees in the Admissions Office, would YOU read 6,000 personal statements? Get real! So they just add up the scores and they're out of there by 3:30. Then why do the law schools ask you to provide all that other personal information? Because if you knew that your low scores were the only thing that mattered, you might not apply, and, frankly, they could use the fifty bucks. Multiply fifty bucks times 6,000 applications, and you can begin to see their point.

Anyway, after submitting the applications, you receive several letters saying, "CONGRATULATIONS!!! You are on the 'hold' list for getting on the 'preliminary waiting list' to be considered for admission." They want to make sure that they can fill their class and get the tuition money they need, so they won't reject you until after they see how many students show up on the first day of class. I mean, what does it hurt them if you give up your other career plans and lifelong ambitions, right? Do you want to go to law school or not? Okay, then stop whining.

Then, finally, you get accepted. But brace yourself. You don't go through law school; law school goes through you. You will never be the same. Don't say I didn't warn you.

4

The First Day

On the first day, all the first-year students gather in the auditorium for the welcoming assembly. You feel exactly like you did on the first day of kindergarten, except that you are not carrying a Bert-and-Ernie lunchbox.

The dean, a grizzled old grizzly[6] with a mossy beard, stands up. You are sure that photosynthesis is occurring in his beard. This is what a law school dean looks like. Half animal and half vegetable. The Swamp Thing. The dean steps to the podium. He asks, "How many people like it better *with* the microphone?" A few hands go up. "How many people like it better *without* the microphone?" A few hands go up. A student shouts out, "How many people don't like it *either way?*" Almost all the hands go up.

With his acute powers of observation, the dean can see that the students are anxious—mostly because swarms of them are either clinging to the ceiling, or passing out in the aisles from hyperventilation. He graciously and soothingly tries to help everyone to relax relax relax. He tells them, for example, how several of last year's flunk-outs have actually been able to pick up the pieces and have meaningful lives anyway. Some people are able

[6] Some would say grisly.

to say just the right thing at the right time, and the dean has that gift.

The dean then introduces the members of the faculty, who are sitting in attack formation at the front of the room. As he names the faculty members in alphabetical order, each professor stands up and glowers menacingly at the students. The dean recites a VERY long list of accomplishments and honors pertaining to each professor. This is generally pretty interesting, at least until you get into the middle of the names beginning with "B," but by then it has become an ordeal similar to the ancient (but effective) "dripping water" torture. Regrettably, there are twenty-four letters of the alphabet to go.

The dean jokes, "Professor Snizzle graduated from this law school with the highest GPA ever achieved. And as long as he is on the faculty, he's going to make sure that it stays that way." Everyone laughs. Everyone, that is, except Professor Snizzle. You check your registration materials. Uh-oh. Professor Snizzle for Property, section 1.

The dean then gives his "Welcoming Speech," in which he admonishes students about the absolute paramount importance of ethics in the practice of law. Given the absolute paramount importance of this issue, this is only the first time that you will hear about it. The second time will be in a speech at your graduation.

At the end of his speech, the dean encourages everyone to gather on the patio for the Gala Sloppy Joe Extravaganza. He says that he always enjoys this luncheon because, if it weren't for this annual event, he would have no social life at all. For some reason, you don't find this particularly difficult to believe. You also realize that it will soon become true for you, too. About the most excitement you will have in the next three years will be to buy the barbecue-flavored Pringles instead of the regular flavor. Whoopee.

CHAPTER
5

The First Year

Remember those horror movies in which somebody wearing a hockey mask terrorizes people at a summer camp and slowly and carefully slashes them all into bloody little pieces? That's what the first year of law school is like. Except that it's worse, because the professors don't wear hockey masks, and you have to look directly at their faces.

At first it's not so bad. You get to read a semi-interesting medieval case in which somebody says, "Forsooth, were it not that Birnam Wood had come to Dunsinane, I would unseam thee from the nave to the chaps." But the honeymoon ends when you have to go to your first class.

The professor has a black belt in an ancient martial art called "the Socratic method." This form of mayhem has nothing to do with the technique by which Socrates gently sought to have his students teach themselves the truth hidden inside each of them. The only connection that the law school version of the Socratic method has with education is that it teaches you to *hate the sound of your own name*. After the professor completely dismantles a student for sheer sport and humiliates several dozen others, he then points out forty-seven different things in the two-paragraph case that you failed to see and still don't understand. You leave class hoping that maybe there is still a job opening at your brother-in-law's toothpick recycling factory. You learn why law school has been compared to a besieged city: everybody outside wants in, and everybody inside wants out.

The professor usually calls on a different student each day. However, Professor Charles Thaddeus Terry, who taught at Columbia at the turn of the century, once called on the same student every day for four months because of the liveliness of the response. This is a true story. Lawyer's honor.

To enable them to call on students, professors require students to sign an enormous seating chart. A student might try to avoid getting called on by not signing the seating chart, but this is not a recommended strategy. She will discover that throughout the semester other people—who are also hiding from the professor—will persistently sit in her "empty" seat instead of in their own seats. So students have devised other ingenious methods to reduce the chances of getting called on—like writing their names upside-down, or in infinitesimally tiny letters that can be read only with an electron microscope. Assuming that professors will avoid calling on names that are long or difficult to pronounce, students with common names sometimes elaborate their names—as in "Michael Brown-Momrath-Outgrabe-Okefenokee-Endoplasmic-Reticulum-Stratford-on-Avon, Jr." However, students who do this should be prepared to have their professor call them something slightly less elegant, like, "Hey, you in the blue shirt." Lastly, some students write the name of someone else—usually a prominent jurist—instead of their own on the seating chart. Rumor has it that someone named "Billy Rehnquist" has flunked out of countless law schools for attending classes but never taking his final exams.

Many students write "case briefs," or one-page summaries of the cases, before class, in case the professor calls on them. This is a good strategy if you have the slightest aversion to utter humiliation. The brain is a truly wonderful thing: it works from the instant you awake until you go to sleep, and it doesn't stop until the moment you are called on in class, when it suffers a complete and immediate core melt-down. You feel like Curly of the Three Stooges: "I try to think, but nothing happens." Your

professor and 150 other students are waiting patiently for you to state the facts of a given case, and the only sound in the room is a low gurgling rattle coming from the back of your throat. Many students brief cases only during the first year, but a guy I know (believe it or not) briefed every single case all three years. Between him and me, we briefed half the cases.

The key to the Socratic method is that the professor never reveals what the answer is. He keeps insisting that THERE IS NO ANSWER. Consistent with this view, he spends the whole class asking questions that no one even begins to understand. To get the answers, you have to buy commercial outlines, which cost $16.95 apiece, and which are published by the same people who publish Cliffs Notes and Key Comics. The commercial outlines are written by the professors and provide them with a handsome income on the side. To insure that you will buy them, the professors tell you that, whatever you do, DO NOT buy any commercial outlines, because they will make it TOO EASY for you, and you will not develop the analytical skills and hard-work ethic that law school is supposed to teach. Pretty cagey, those professors.

There are lots of different commercial outlines and other study aids available: Gillies, Nut Books, etc. Although they are produced by many different publishers, all study aids have two things in common:

1. They contradict what your professor said in class.
2. They contradict each other.

So they're all equally effective.

At the beginning the people in your class seem like nice enough folks. But gradually everyone begins to realize that their only hope of getting a job is to blast the chromosomes out of their classmates in the giant zero-sum thermonuclear war game called "class standing." Class standing is what saves law school from being a boring, cooperative learning experience and makes it the dynamic, exciting, survival-of-the-fittest, cutthroatly competitive, grueling treadmill of unsurpassed joy that it is. In other words, it begins to prepare you for law practice.

Class standing does irreparable psychic damage and scars bright and creative people for the rest of their natural lives. A bright and creative person is about to do something bright and creative in her life, but then she thinks, "No, I was only number 67 out of 150 in my class, and I'm probably not capable of any mental activity greater than picking slugs off zucchini plants." So she doesn't do anything.

To make sure that the message gets through, the professors are not content with the demeaning and humiliating exercise of calculating class standing. No. First, they tell students that class standing and grades do not matter. Not at all. They know that the students will remember the episode with the commercial outlines and will therefore conclude that nothing else in the entire universe matters except class standing and grades. Then, to strike the final blow, the professors adopt a grading system straight out of the ninth circle of Dante's *Inferno*. They take students who have undergraduate GPA's of A-minus, and who have never gotten a B-minus in their entire life, and they give them—get this—all C's!!! This will prove that the professors know the law better than the students, in case the point was somehow overlooked.

Most law students never recover from this act of evil genius, and they spend the rest of their lives figuring out how to get even with the rest of humanity. This consuming desire for vengeance is called "appropriate lawyerly zeal."

This is the reason that Supreme Court justices are always so testy with each other in their opinions. An example: The majority writes, "When two of our esteemed colleagues left the majority and joined the dissent, it raised the average IQ in both groups by thirty points." Ha! The dissent responds, "The majority wanted to prevail in the worst way, and the Court's opinion is the worst way it could think of." So there. The justices are still hopping mad about that C-minus they got in Civil Procedure forty years ago.

During the first year, the law students quickly divide into three groups:

The Active Participants: Overconfident geeks who compete with each other to take up the most airtime pointing out that before law school, when they were Fulbright Scholars, they thought of a question marginally relevant to today's discussion. Their names appear on the class's "Turkey Bingo" cards, a game you win if five people on your card speak during one class period. The Active Participants stop talking completely when first-semester grades come out and they get all C's.

The Backbenchers: Cool dudes who "opt out" of law school's competitive culture and never prepare for class. They sit on the back row, rather than in their assigned seats, so the professor can't find them on the seating chart. They ask if they can "borrow" your class outline.

The Terrified Middle Group: People who spend most of their time wondering what the hey is going on, and why don't the professors just tell us what the law is and stop playing "hide the ball" and shrouding the law in mystery/philosophy/sociology/nihilistic relativism/astrology/voodoo/sadomasochistic Socratic kung fu?

The first-year curriculum consists of Legal Writing and five substantive law courses:

Civil Procedure. In this class you will learn about the paper wars of litigation. You will discover why, every time a case is filed, another forest dies.

Contracts. You will study rules based on a model of two-fisted negotiators with equal bargaining power who dicker freely, voluntarily agree on all terms, and reduce their understanding to a writing intended to embody their full agreement. You will learn that the last contract fitting this model was signed in 1879.

Criminal Law. Here you will study common law crimes that haven't been the law anywhere for more than 100 years. Then, to bring things up to date, you will study the Model Penal Code, which is not the law anywhere today.

Property. You will learn about "livery of seisin" and similar laws governing clods. Some of these legal rules are simply incomprehensible. For example, according to the California Supreme Court, nobody can be expected to understand the Rule Against Perpetuities.[7]

Torts. You will study a compensation system in which the transaction costs generally exceed the payments to the injured parties. Fortunately, most of the transaction costs occur in the form of attorney's fees.

The cases are, of course, dreadfully boring. However, there are a few interesting characters you meet in the legal literature, like the "fertile octogenarian," the "naked trespasser," and the "officious intermeddler." It is best to keep these three people from spending much unsupervised time together. Also, there are

[7] *See* Lucas v. Hamm, 364 P.2d 685 (Cal. 1961).

a few interesting cases, like *Cordas v. Peerless Transportation Co.*,[8] in which the judge was apparently a frustrated playwright:

> This case presents the ordinary man—that problem child of the law—in a most bizarre setting. As a lonely chauffeur in defendant's employ he became in a trice the protagonist in a breath-bating drama with a denouement almost tragic. It appears that a man, whose identity it would be indelicate to divulge, was feloniously relieved of his portable goods by two nondescript highwaymen in an alley near 26th Street and Third Avenue, Manhattan; they induced him to relinquish his possessions by a strong argument ad hominem couched in the convincing cant of the criminal and pressed at the point of a most persuasive pistol. Laden with their loot, but not thereby impeded, they took an abrupt departure, and he, shuffling off the coil of that discretion which enmeshed him in the alley, quickly gave chase . . . .

The judge was obviously having such a good time it's hard to believe that the point of all this humor was (chuckle chuckle) to hand down a decision *against a woman and her infant children who were injured by a runaway taxi.*[9]

Another example is *Fisher v. Lowe*,[10] in which the plaintiff sued the defendants for damaging his beautiful oak tree with an automobile. The trial court held that the defendants were immune from liability under the no-fault insurance act. The Michigan Court of Appeals held:

> We thought that we would never see
> A suit to compensate a tree.
>
> A suit whose claim in tort is prest
> Upon a mangled tree's behest;
>
> A tree whose battered trunk was prest
> Against a Chevy's crumpled crest;

[8] 27 N.Y.S.2d 198 (N.Y. City Ct. 1941).
[9] *Id.* at 200.
[10] 333 N.W.2d 67 (Mich. App. 1983).

A tree that faces each new day
With bark and limb in disarray;

A tree that may forever bear
A lasting need for tender care.

Flora lovers though we three,
We must uphold the court's decree.

Affirmed.

Justice Jackson once listed some humorous ways that judges declined to follow their own prior opinions:

> Baron Bramwell extricated himself . . . by saying, "The matter does not appear to me now as it appears to have appeared to me then." . . . Lord Westbury, . . . it is said, rebuffed a barrister's reliance upon an earlier opinion of his Lordship: "I can only say that I am amazed that a man of my intelligence should have been guilty of giving such an opinion."[11]

A strange case is *United States ex rel. Mayo v. Satan and his Staff*,[12] in which the plaintiff sued Satan under federal statutes for violating his civil rights. He alleged that the defendant had on numerous occasions caused him misery and unwarranted threats, placed deliberate obstacles in his path, and caused his downfall, and therefore had deprived him of his constitutional rights. The court denied the plaintiff's application to proceed in forma pauperis, holding:

> We question whether plaintiff may obtain personal jurisdiction over the defendant in this judicial district. The complaint contains no allegation of residence in this district. While the official reports disclose no case where this defendant has appeared as defendant there is an unofficial account of a trial in New Hampshire where this defendant filed an action of mortgage foreclosure as plaintiff. The defendant in that action was rep-

---

[11] McGrath v. Kristensen, 340 U.S. 162, 178 (1950) (Jackson, J., concurring).
[12] 54 F.R.D. 282 (W.D. Pa. 1971).

resented by the preeminent advocate of the day, and raised the defense that the plaintiff was a foreign prince with no standing to sue in an American Court. This defense was overcome by overwhelming evidence to the contrary. Whether or not this would raise an estoppel in the present case we are unable to determine at this time.

. . . .

We note that the plaintiff has failed to include with his complaint the required form of instructions for the United States Marshal for directions as to service of process.

The plaintiff sued without a lawyer, because suing the devil would present lawyers with an obvious conflict of interest.

These are some of the interesting cases. But most cases are, to paraphrase Mark Twain, chloroform in print. The latest casebooks actually have a pocket part containing smelling salts.

Last but not most, I advise against becoming romantically involved with anyone in your law school class. Your time is much too precious for such frivolities as friendship, love, and meaning. And if *your* time is not too precious for those things, it will be for the person in whom you are interested. Your dating life will likely resemble topics studied in the second half of Contracts: Misunderstanding, Repudiation, Frustration, and Excuse.

So that's what the first year is like. Unfortunately, the first year is the best year of law school. The three years of law school are similar to the three kinds of rocks:

The first year: Igneous. You are on fire.
The second year: Metamorphic. Tremendous pressures change you dramatically.
The third year: Sedimentary. Yawn.

If you stayed in law school any longer, you would become fossilized. Just look at your professors.

CHAPTER

6

The Law Faculty

If you want to know what kind of people law professors are, ask yourself this question: "What kind of a person would give up a salary of a jillion dollars a year in a big firm to drive a rusted-out Ford Pinto and wear suits made out of old horse blankets?" Think about this carefully before asking your professor's opinion on any subject.

A law professor is a person whose greatest aspiration is to be like Professor Kingsfield in the movie *The Paper Chase*. When Professor Kingsfield died, he donated his heart for transplantation. The hospital charged an outrageous sum for the heart. It justified the price on the theory that the heart had never been used.

One professor who saw *The Paper Chase* decided (this is a true story) to act out one of the scenes from the film in his class. He called on a student, who replied that he was unprepared. The professor said, "Mr. Jones, come down here." The student walked all the way down to the front of the class. The professor gave the student a dime, and said, "Take this dime. Call your mother. Tell her that your chances of ever becoming a lawyer are seriously in doubt." Ashamed, the student turned and walked slowly toward the door. Suddenly, however, he had a flash of inspiration. He turned around, and in a loud voice, said, "NO,

Clyde. [He called the professor by his first name.] I have a BETTER idea! YOU take this dime, and you go call ALL YOUR FRIENDS!!!" The class broke into pandemonium. The professor broke the student into little bitty pieces.

Politics are often divisive at law schools. In the 1960's the faculties were conservative and the students were liberal. In the 1980's the students were conservative and the faculties were liberal—the professors having spent their formative years wearing love beads and attending Grateful Dead concerts. The 1970's were a difficult transitional period during which, for an awkward moment, faculties and students were able to communicate. They discovered that they did not like each other.

When law professors are not doing important things like writing commercial outlines, they are writing casebooks. Of course, they make you buy their casebook for their class. One of the cardinal rules of casebooks is that they must have as many authors as there are soldiers in the Montana National Guard. For example, a well known casebook is Druid, Crustacean, Headswell, Schmo, Vacuous & Geekman, *Cases, Materials, and Inscrutable Footnotes on Doozle and Hornbeagle's Law of Rural Chicken Diseases* (9th ed. 1992). The publisher recruited six authors so that the book would be adopted in six classes. The book costs $59.95, but it's not a total loss. At the end of the year, the bookstore will buy it back for $3.87.

Law professors spend a lot of time writing because law schools have adopted the rule of "publish or perish." That's why law professors' "office hours" for student consultation have been reduced to "office nanoseconds." It's also why your school keeps professors whose classroom performance consists entirely of mumbling inaudibly and soaking the front of their clothes with drool. They add to the prestige of the school by writing impenetrable tomes about such subjects as the law of insect matrimony. These books are read by three people in the entire world, two of whom are the professor's children.

Law schools claim that their promotion and tenure criteria also include citizenship and teaching ability, but this is a ruse. "Good

citizenship" means "no indictments."[13] "Good teaching ability" means that the teacher can explain how to sign the seating chart. One professor left the dean's office and puzzled, "Did the dean say that I am noted for my humorous delivery, or humored for my notorious delivery?"

It's not completely the law professors' fault, however. They have no training *whatsoever* in teaching. Law school deans claim that attending law school itself is enough to qualify a person to teach law school. Fortunately, we don't hire our elementary school teachers that way. We require extensive training in education before we let anyone stand even in front of a kindergarten class. This is true at every level of the educational system except where teaching is the most complicated—the university. There, we let everyone wing it.

The law faculty can be divided into three groups:

[13] Or, at some schools, "no convictions."

1. The Youngsters. Hip, nucleomagnetic surges of energy. At least, they *think* they're hip. They're actually about as hip as Elmer Fudd singing the music of Janet Jackson.

   Clothing: Indistinguishable from the students'.

   Hobby: Having multiple panic attacks about getting tenure.

   Students call them by: Their first names.

2. The Middle-Agers. Sixty-watt bulbs who consider themselves to be airport searchlights. Law professors have enormous egos. Question: What's the fastest way to die? Answer: Get between a law professor and a camera.

   Clothing: Rumpled tweed and Hush Puppies.

   Hobby: Complaining that if it just weren't for all those students, university life would be okay.

   Students call them by: Their last names.

3. The Senior Faculty.

   Clothing: Elephant molt.

   Hobby: Sitting in their office with the light off. They were *not* sleeping, they explain when you knock on their door. They just have sensitive eyes.

   Students call them by: Their name, which they can't remember at the moment.

However, you won't get to know the professors very well. Faculty-student relations are very distant, mostly because the student-faculty ratio is so high. Law school is like a Cecil B. DeMille movie: a cast of thousands, wandering in the desert. Because it can be done in such large numbers, legal education is the cheapest form of graduate education. For some unknown reason, however, the savings are not passed on to the students.

To try to prove that at heart they are really gentle, fun-loving people, professors will occasionally do something a little bit zany, like wear a costume to class on Halloween. This makes the students laugh and cheer. Before you laugh and cheer, however, you should check your calendar. It is often difficult to tell whether a professor is wearing a costume or not.

All of this leads to one question: If getting into law teaching is so highly competitive, why aren't the professors any better than banana slugs with hair? This is one of the secret mysteries of the law.

CHAPTER

7

A Day in the Life

Here is a typical day in the life of a law student:

7:00 A.M. Alarm clock goes off. Hit snooze button. Go back to sleep.

7:10 A.M. Alarm clock goes off. Hit snooze button. Go back to sleep.

7:20 A.M. Alarm clock goes off. Throw alarm clock across room. Go back to sleep.

8:00 A.M. Wake up in a panic. Wonder why your alarm clock didn't go off.

Your head feels like you've been bungee-jumping with a too-long cord. Take a quick shower. Look in the mirror and wince. Feel stubble on face (if male) or legs (if female). Decide that you can make it one more day without shaving. Gingerly select some clothes from the decomposing pile on the floor and get dressed. Gulp down breakfast, which consists of a glass of orange juice and the last remaining slice of pizza from the pizza delivery order last week. Or was it last month? Try to guess whether the pizza was originally anchovy or Canadian bacon. The legal realists

asserted that the law depends on what the judge ate for breakfast. What if you don't even know what you ate for breakfast?

8:30 A.M. Catch the bus that goes to the law school. Wonder
why your alarm clock didn't go off. Sleep.

9:00 A.M. Contracts class. The classroom is half empty, but
will fill up during the next twenty minutes. Students gradually stumble in, huddling over Styrofoam cups of coffee
like zeks in a gulag. You're grateful that you don't look as
bad as they do. You stroke your stubble.

Professor Freeble sets his class notes on the podium and blows
the dust off. A huge cloud of dust fills the room. He then calls on
a student and asks him to recite the facts of *Dougherty v. Salt*,[14]
a classic contracts case.

In the case, Aunt Tillie said that she would take care of her
eight-year-old nephew Charley. The boy's guardian accused
Aunt Tillie of being all "show" and no "go." So Aunt Tillie, in
a huff, signed a promissory note to pay $3,000 to Charley. Then
she had the bad timing to die before she paid the debt, and the
executrix of her estate refused to pay it, probably because of the
minor technicality that if she did the beneficiaries of the estate
would have sued her socks off.

PROFESSOR: Should the estate be liable to pay the debt?

STUDENT: Yes. Aunt Tillie made a promise, and promises
should be kept.

PROFESSOR: Suppose your parents promise you some new skis
for your birthday. Your birthday comes, but there are no
skis. Do you sue your parents? [Laughter from class.]

STUDENT: I guess not.

PROFESSOR: You seem to have a firm grasp of the obvious.
[Laughter.] Now try to engage in some straight thinking.
Straight thinking is generally preferred, based on the as-

---

[14] 125 N.E. 94 (N.Y. 1919).

sumption that we live in a Euclidean universe.[15] [Laughter.]

Aunt Tillie's promise was merely a promise to make a gift, was it not? There was no consideration.

STUDENT: What's consideration?

PROFESSOR: It will be nice to have a familiar face in class next year. [Laughter.]

I will ask the questions. In law school you will teach yourself the law. If you don't teach yourself the law, then I feel guilty when I draw my paycheck. [Laughter.]

Law school scratches your eyes out, and then it scratches them back in again. You arrive here with a skull full of mush,[16] and you leave here thinking like lawyers.

I'll give you another chance. In this battle of wits, it's not fair to pick on an unarmed person. [Laughter.]

---

[15] *Cf.* Euclid v. Ambler Realty Co., 272 U.S. 365 (1926) (implicitly assuming that every point on the surface of a sphere is unique). *But cf.* Laurence H. Tribe, *The Curvature of Constitutional Space: What Lawyers Can Learn from Modern Physics,* 103 Harv. L. Rev. 1 (1989).

[16] *Cf.* cannibal conventions, where people arrive with a mush full of skulls.

STUDENT [looking at his notes]: I think that consideration is the *quid pro quo*. It's what is given in exchange for something else. It's what makes a transaction a bargain, an economic exchange.

PROFESSOR: Oh, really?

STUDENT: And this class is definitely none of those things. I pay my tuition and I have to teach myself the law. So, according to your argument, I should get my tuition refunded.

PROFESSOR: And we thought that the hole in the ozone layer was not yet having any demonstrable effects. [Laughter.] Next time you will give a report to the class on whether executed gifts can be rescinded. Research materials may be found in the library. The rest of you (my little pretties) can read pages 73–126. [Cackle.] Class dismissed.

What a headbanger of a teacher, you think. This class is like mental slam dancing. No, it's more like playing right field in a baseball game. There are long periods of boredom, interrupted by moments of sheer terror. And only the professor knows if there even *is* a ball. Freeble seems to take delight in tormenting students. You might be getting paranoid, you tell yourself. But it doesn't matter. Freeble hates paranoids and nonparanoids alike.

10:00 A.M. Go to the library and study. Mark your casebook with multiple highlighter pens to create the illusion of being organized. Use green ink to mark the facts, blue ink to mark the law, and yellow ink to mark the interesting parts of the case. Realize that you will never run out of yellow ink.

11:00 A.M. Property class. More slash and burn. Today's subject is an ancient English case that has been irrelevant for several hundred years. The only way this information could conceivably be useful is if time travel were perfected by the time you graduated and you decided to practice law in fifteenth-century Britain.

A student volunteers to recite a case. A volunteer is like one of those birds that pick leeches out of an alligator's mouth.[17] Because it needs the bird to perform this task, the alligator opens its mouth wide and does not harm the bird. Law professors, by contrast, gently roll students around on their tongues, lure them further inside, and then SNAP their jaws shut. Then the law professors can't figure out why after a few weeks students stop volunteering. Law professors are not as smart as their reptile cousins, alligators.

12:00 noon. Lunch. You buy a balanced lunch from the four major food groups: the Hostess Ding Dong group, the barbecue-flavored potato chip group, the Cheetos group, and the cola group. You consume them slowly to allow the carbohydrates to react chemically in synergistic ways. This is the high point of the day.

1:00 P.M. Civil Procedure. Nobody understands Civil Procedure. To make matters worse, the professor is a space cadet, only occasionally coming within the earth's gravitational pull. The musical theme from *The Twilight Zone* keeps running through your mind. Dee dee dee dee, dee dee dee dee.

You write on your paper:

This is your brain: O
This is your brain in Civil Procedure: ·
Any questions?

One person seems to be understanding what is going on: the techno-geek sitting directly behind you. His T-shirt says "Hard Disk Cafe." He's typing furiously on his laptop computer. It's called a laptop because it's supposed to sit on somebody's lap, as opposed to where it's really sitting, which is three inches behind your left ear. The clickety-clack of the keyboard is rapidly turning you into a crazoid. You finally grasp the laptop and turn it around so you can read the brilliant notes he has written. You see that he has gotten to the fourth world on Super Mario Brothers III.

---

[17] Yuck! But they really do it.

2:00 P.M. Go to the library to study. After much searching, you find an empty carrel and sit down. You read the graffiti on the wall next to the carrel: "Spock. I think we've beamed inside a wall." All right. You are a Trekkie yourself. The latest Star Trek movie is your favorite even though, halfway through the film, Mr. Spock has to do the Vulcan Mind Meld just to discover whether the movie has any plot. You almost gave up on Star Trek when you saw some photographs of a Star Trek convention. It was full of middle-aged people dressed in their pajamas. They looked like they still live in their parents' basement. You separate the second and third fingers on your right hand. Live long and make megabucks.

Got to concentrate on your studies. Make a list of things to do:

Read and brief all cases for tomorrow.
Finish library research exercises.
Write first draft of legal research memo.
Outline all courses from the beginning of the semester.

What a staggering load! Just thinking about it makes you tired. You lay your head down on your open casebook.

3:00 P.M. You wake up and try to lift your head off your book. Your face is fused to the open page of your book with drool. You use your pencil to pry yourself free. You look at your watch and panic. Time for Criminal Law. You rush to class.

Professor Pounder is the teacher. Robo-Prof. In his next life, he is hoping to come back as a human being. He quickly destroys a student in an act of random but efficient violence. You wonder whether you should outline the student in body chalk.

You are gradually developing a tough exoskeleton so that nothing a professor says can hurt your feelings. "But why should *I* be the one with the exoskeleton?" you ask yourself. "It's the *professors* who are the invertebrates."

4:00 P.M. Time for study group. The purpose of the study group is to help one another, but all you are usually able to accomplish is the rearrangement of ignorance. The study group has five other students in it, each with a unique personality. They are like the stereotypical actors in a World War II movie:

Tony: The street-smart kid from Brooklyn. Before the movie is over, he will die throwing a hand grenade into a machine-gun nest of law professors.

Monica: The former university professor who decided to become a lawyer and make a living instead of having a life.

Skeeter: The big galoot straight off the farm. Because he got married in Nebraska, people threw corn instead of rice. That's why he didn't get married in Idaho.

Elaine: A bright student who hates law professors with a passion. She will eventually turn traitor and become one.

Wilfred: The 200-megabyte genius. He has no contact with reality. He and the others in the group have a strangely symbiotic relationship. He helps them to understand the most complex and abstract jurisprudential aspects of the law. In return, they remind him to put his shoes on in the morning.

The study group meeting is productive. It lasts one hour, which is 2.25 hours in lawyer billable hours. The group exchanges critical information about the latest law school gossip, the cheapest restaurants in the city, and the starting salaries at the big law firms. The second half is a prolonged but ultimately successful discussion about when the next meeting will be. Well, at least you got *something* done.

5:00 P.M. Study for tomorrow's classes.

8:00 P.M. Start working on your legal research memo. Outlining your courses will have to wait. After all, there's plenty of time left. Remember your motto: "The sooner you get behind, the more time you have to catch up. Do it today!"

10:00 P.M. Catch the last bus home to your apartment. You look at the mess in your apartment. It reflects the Second Law of Thermodynamics: the entropy of the universe tends to a maximum. Your apartment is leading the way toward total chaos.

10:30 P.M. You realize that you have missed dinner, so you open the refrigerator to see what's there. There's half a bottle of milk, some meatloaf with hair growing on it, and a jar of horseradish. You wonder if horseradish is an effective disinfectant for meatloaf hair. You decide not.

You look in the freezer. Sticks de la fish? Nope. Too fancy. You take the milk out of the refrigerator and pour it over a bowl of Coco Puffs. You'll make sure to get a decent meal tomorrow. Also, you remember that you need to get some exercise. A while ago you went to the gym to lift weights, but the laughter made it difficult to concentrate.

You study while you eat. The tenant in the apartment directly above yours starts practicing his bagpipes. Wonderful. Studies have shown that it is virtually impossible to distinguish the music of a world-class bagpipe band from the sound made by 300 cats and a blowtorch.

12:00 midnight. Time to get ready for bed. You look in the mirror and see that there is a reverse image of the page from your torts casebook printed on the side of your face. Great. NO WONDER your study group was looking at you funny.

12:15 A.M. Bed. Got to get up earlier tomorrow. You locate your alarm clock and set it for 6:00 A.M. You wonder whether it will go off.

You sleep like a baby: you snooze for an hour, wake up and cry for a while, and then snooze some more.

You have a dream in which a genie appears and grants you one wish. You ask for peace in the Middle East. The genie asks to see a map of the Middle East. He points to the map and explains that, given the location of the various countries, achieving peace in the area is impossible. He asks you to make another wish, so you wish for a happy and fulfilling law school experience. The genie pauses and asks, "Could I have another look at the map again?"

6:00 A.M. Your alarm clock goes off. You hit the snooze button.

CHAPTER
8

Legal Writing

During your first year, you take a class called Legal Writing. The sole objective of this class is to make you write like real lawyers as little as possible. Lawyers write as if they were paid by the word, or maybe even as if they were born in a parallel universe. For example, here is the legal translation that has been offered for the simple everyday phrase, "I give you this orange."

Know all men by these presents that I hereby give, grant, bargain, sell, release, convey, transfer, and quitclaim all my right, title, interest, benefit, and use whatever in, of, and concerning this chattel, known as an orange, or citrus orantium, together with all the appurtenances thereto of skin, pulp, pip, rind, seeds, and juice for his own use and behoof, to himself and his heirs in fee simple forever, free from all liens, encumbrances, easements, limitations, restraints, or conditions whatsoever, any and all prior deeds, transfers or other documents whatsoever, now or anywhere made to the contrary notwithstanding, with full power to bite, cut, suck, or otherwise eat the said orange or to give away the same, with or without its skin, pulp, pip, rind, seeds, or juice.[18]

---

[18] Plain Wayne [pseud.], Wis. Bar Bull., Feb. 1975, at 61.

This kind of supernatural incantation is designed to perpetuate the perceived mysticism of the law and its official high priests. However, legal writing teachers tell you that it is preferable to use concise language and simple, everyday words. Benjamin Franklin said, "Never use a long word when a short one will do." Of course, he was a printer, and he had to set the type by hand. Naturally, he preferred "pay" over "remuneration."

Lawyers like to use "lawyerisms," like "aforementioned," "hereinafter," and "mortgagee." However, most people can't understand legalese. When the loan officer asked Archie Bunker if his home was encumbered, he replied, "No, it's stucco and wood." As Charles Beardsley said, "The writer who uses words unknown to his reader might as well bark."[19] So remember the words of the ditty:

> When promulgating your esoteric cogitations and articulating your superficial sentimentalities, beware of platitudinous ponderosity. Let your extemporaneous verbal evaporations and expatiations have lucidity and intelligibility without rodomontade or thespian bombast. Avoid innocuous vacuity, pompous propensity, and vaniloquent vapidity.

Lawyers do strange things to language. For instance, they add "-ize" to all sorts of words. They don't say "use"; they say "utilize." They also say "actualize," "initialize," and "prioritize." If you ask me, it's enough to make you "externalize" your breakfast. They should try harder to "laypersonize" their language.

Lawyers also write "said" a lot. For example, one complaint stated:

> "[B]eginning at a point on SAID railroad track about a half a mile or more north of a point opposite SAID curve in SAID highway, large quantities of highly volatile coal were unneces-

---

[19] *The Difference Between Writing and Yelping,* Cal. Law., Oct. 1989, at 136 (quoting an editorial in the *San Francisco Chronicle* (1941)).

sarily thrown into the firebox of SAID locomotive and upon the fire contained therein, thereby preventing proper combustion of SAID coal, resulting in great clouds of dense smoke being emitted from the smokestack of SAID locomotive." . . . [Defendant] knew SAID smoke would "fall upon and cover SAID curve in SAID highway when SAID engine reached a point on SAID railroad tracks opposite SAID curve, unless SAID smoke was checked in the meantime."[20]

The judges who quoted this language, realizing that they had not yet used up their daily quota, then added another sentence containing eight more "saids." Said practice is supposedly invoked for precision, but said precision is illusory. Since the author referred to only one locomotive, "said" is unnecessary. If he had referred to two, "said" wouldn't tell you which one.[21] The real problem is that "the" doesn't sound important enough to lawyers, so they instead write said "saids."

Another sin of legal writing is verbosity. This problem has been around for centuries. In 1596 an English chancellor made

---

[20] Button v. Pennsylvania Ry. Co., 57 N.E.2d 444, 445 (Ind. App. 1944) (en banc) (emphasis added).

[21] Richard C. Wydick, *Plain English for Lawyers*, 66 Cal. L. Rev. 727, 740 (1978).

an example of a wordy 120-page document by ordering that a hole be cut in it, the writer's head be stuffed in the hole, and the writer be led around and exhibited to all those attending court at Westminster Hall.[22]

One example of verbosity is the practice of using pairs of duplicative words, like "cease and desist," "null and void," "free and clear," "suffer and permit," "devise and bequeath," and "idiot and professor." This practice supposedly stems from periods in history when English lawyers had two languages to choose from: first, Celtic and Anglo-Saxon, then English and Latin, and later English and French. Who knows for sure whether this is true and correct? It sure creates a lot of redundancy and duplication.

A few judges have pursued the virtue of conciseness with a passion. For example, a taxpayer in the U.S. Tax Court testified, "As God is my judge, I do not owe this tax." Judge Murdock replied, "He's not, I am; you do."[23] Another example is *Denny v. Radar Industries*.[24] Most of the opinion states, "The appellant has attempted to distinguish the factual situation in this case from that in [a prior case]. He didn't. We couldn't. Affirmed."

Another common booboo in legal writing is the mixed metaphor. This is a figure of speech that begins with one image and then, as slick as Elvis's hair grease, shifts to another. For example, a bar association committee reported that it had "smelled a rat and nipped it in the bud."[25] Donald Nixon complained, "People are using Watergate as a political football to bury my brother."[26] Even Jiminy Cricket told Pinocchio, "You buttered your bread—now sleep in it." Therefore, before using a mixed metaphor wedded to the very fabric of your argument, be sure to run it up the flagpole of microscopic scrutiny. Otherwise, the

---

[22] *Id.* at 727.

[23] Henry Weihofen, *Legal Writing Style* 41 (2d ed. 1980).

[24] 184 N.W.2d 289 (Mich. App. 1971).

[25] *See* Gyles Brandreth, *The Joy of Lex* 227 (1980) (quoting Boyle Roche).

[26] Gertrude Block, *Effective Legal Writing* 42 (2d ed. 1983).

sacred cows will come home to roost with a vengeance.[27] But I'm skating on hot water, so I'll move on.

Lawyers also use a lot of clichés. They say things like "The case is open and shut. Don't cut off your nose to spite your face." And "To think that you will escape the day of reckoning in the cold light of reason is the height of absurdity barking up the wrong tree." So bite the bullet and avoid old clichés like the plague. As Samuel Goldwyn said, "Let's have some new clichés."

Legal writing also often uses double negatives. The United States Supreme Court has truly refined this art, writing the world's first and only—believe or not—QUADRUPLE negative:

> This is not to say, however, that the prima facie case may not be met by evidence supporting a finding that a lesser degree of segregated schooling in the core city area would not have resulted even if the board had not acted as it did.[28]

Government cryptographers have been trying to decipher this sentence for years. So far, they have been able to tell that it has something to do with schools.

In legal writing you are also introduced to the two computerized systems of legal research, Lexis and Westlaw. These systems permit you to find hundreds of cases merely by pushing a button. This allows you to avoid packing musty case reporters up and down the stairs of the library, which would interrupt your completely sedentary lifestyle. It's much better to exercise those finger muscles and let the rest of your body atrophy into a shapeless blob of protoplasm.

Lexis and Westlaw are very convenient, but they do have limitations. For example, suppose you want to find all the cases

---

[27] Gyles Brandreth, *supra* note 25, at 227. Justice Stewart once wrote, "This case presents a double-barreled dilemma, which in all candor I think the Court's opinion has not succeeded in papering over." Sherbert v. Verner, 374 U.S. 398, 413 (1963) (Stewart, J., concurring).

[28] Keyes v. School Dist. No. 1, 413 U.S. 189, 211 (1973) (Brennan, J.).

in which a lawyer called opposing counsel a "ferret face." Type in the query: counsel /s "ferret face". The computer will respond: "13,759 cases answer your query. Please narrow your search terms." So then you'll have to limit the search terms to "three-eyed ferret face," "banana-nosed ferret face," etc. As you can see, this can be a lot of frustrating work. That's one reason they call that little blinking thing on your computer screen "the cursor."

The second half of your legal writing class is "moot court," a thrilling little death march in which you prepare a hundred-page document that is called, appropriately enough, a "brief."

The moot court problems are always fascinating hypotheticals addressing such stimulating issues as stagnant-water rights in sixteenth-century France. Although your professor tries to make the problem a balanced one, it turns out that your opponent has the law, the facts, and the policy arguments on his side—whereas all you have on your side is your ability to keep from laughing hysterically at your own arguments by sticking a pin into your palm. Never mind. The judges will tell you that the process is fair anyway, because having a really bad case reveals your mettle as an advocate. Then they will give the prize to your opponent.

Moot court gives you the privilege of getting in a heated argument with another student in front of a panel of judges composed of EXTREMELY experienced second- and third-year students who have never set foot inside a courthouse in their lives. After the argument, the judges give you helpful advice. The first judge says, "Don't wave your hands so much." The second judge says, "Use more hand motions." The third judge says, "All the hand motions were okay except when you punched your opponent in the eye. You should have punched him in the mouth."

The worst part of legal writing is having to learn the rules of legal citation. Literally thousands of subrules are set forth in a mutant mass of legalisms called the *Bluebook*. The operating principles of the *Bluebook* are: (1) Nature abhorreth a vacuum; and (2) Anything worth doing is worth overdoing. The first *Bluebook* was a simple booklet that showed how to cite the most commonly used sources. But because the *Bluebook* has insisted on having a rule for every situation imaginable, it has grown enormously (sort of like the Blob, but with a less appealing personality). So now the *Bluebook* describes how to cite such often-used sources as *Vanity Fair* and the Argentine provincial court of labor appeals. The twelfth edition fit in a person's pocket. The current (fifteenth) edition could have its own carrying case. The twentieth edition will undoubtedly arrive on a flatbed truck.

Under the prior *Bluebook*s, when citing books you had to give the initial of the author's first name, but for law review articles you didn't, which I guess was supposed to be some kind of stupid reward for writing books. You were never permitted to give the author's first name for articles, even though there are 4,000 law professors named "Smith." (I have a suspicion that the other law professors who share my surname have been really ticked off[29] at me because of this rule.) However, the newest edition of the *Bluebook* finally consented to giving the author's full name.

The *Bluebook* also contains the official "introductory signals," which lawyers use to introduce citations. The introductory signals have been attacked as

> an ultra vires imposition of a full-blown theory of stare decisis. . . . Use *no signal* when you've got the guts. Use *e.g.* when there are other examples you are too lazy to find or are skeptical of unearthing. Use *accord* when one court has cribbed from the other's opinion. Use *see* when the case is on all three's. Use *cf.* when you've wasted your time reading the case. Insert *but* in front of these last two when a frown instead of a smile is indicated.[30]

However, the *Bluebook* still leaves out some very useful signals, such as *read and weep* and *try to distinguish this one*. For contrary

---

[29] From the German verb *aufticken*.
[30] Peter Lushing, Book Review, 67 Colum. L. Rev. 599, 601 (1967) (reviewing *A Uniform System of Citation* (11th ed. 1967)).

authority, it omits *disregard, ignore also*, and *for a really bizarre view, see.*

The *Bluebook* has rules for everything. It permits legal writing teachers to penalize students for failing to grasp the subtle distinction between a period followed by an ellipsis and an ellipsis followed by a period. It has no fewer than 140 pages of mandatory abbreviations, which means that the space saved by abbreviations is purchased with the time wasted in looking them up. It dictates when numbers must be written as numerals and when they must be spelled out. Inexplicably, the rule is different for footnotes than it is for text, and the general rules are subject to six (6?) exceptions. The *Bluebook* is thick with thin things.

Despite all of this, the editors insist that the current edition of the *Bluebook* is "easier to use."[31] Easier than what? An F-16 fighter jet? Short of that, I'm not sure. But I am sure that studying the *Bluebook* is not likely to overload the pleasure sensors in your brain.

---

[31] *The Bluebook: A Uniform System of Citation* at v (15th ed. 1991).

Exams and Other Fun Stuff

By the end of the semester, you need something to save you from the frenzy of laughter of your law school classes. That's why law schools have final exams.

Studies have shown that the best way to learn is to have frequent exams on small amounts of material and to receive lots of feedback from the teacher. Consequently, law school does none of this. Law school is supposed to be an intellectual challenge. Therefore, law professors give only one exam, the FINAL EXAM OF ARMAGEDDON, and they give absolutely no feedback before then.

Actually, they give no feedback after then, either, because they don't return the exams to the students. A few students go and look at their exam after it is graded, but this is a complete waste of time, unless they just want to see again what they wrote and have a combat-veteran–type flashback of the whole horrific nightmare. The professors never write any comments on the exams. That might permit you to do better next time, which would upset the class ranking.

Some professors are kind enough to distribute a model answer for you to look at. You tell the professor that you can't see any difference whatsoever between your low-scoring exam and the model answer. He replies, "Well, there's your problem."

Another reason that law professors give only one exam is that, basically, they are lazier than comatose three-toed sloths. They teach half as many hours as other professors, are paid twice as much, and get promoted three times as fast. Then they whine like three-year-olds because they have to grade one exam per class. I mean, this is every single semester, year in and year out. The constant grind is enough to kill a person, I tell you.

Since professors won't tell you how to do well on your exams, I will. Because you cover so much material, you need to make an outline for each class. You can do this alone, assuming you have about an extra thousand years to kill. An easier way is for your study group to divide up the classes, with each person outlining one class. This differs from the prior approach in that it is humanly possible. However, you are likely to open up your study group's Contracts outline the night before the exam and find a sentence like this: "An offer is the manifestation of gooberness to enter into a something or other (I didn't catch what the professor said here) so made as to justify another person in understanding that [illegible] is invited and will gyre and gimble in the wabe. Or something like that." You then realize that the classmate who wrote this dropped out six weeks ago and is inaccessible by telephone, and you run screaming around the room like the lunatic that you are. So it's really better just to buy the commercial outline and forget it.

Then, memorize the outline. As you pour it in the top of your head, most of it will run out your ears. Keep scooping up the stuff that runs out your ears and pour it back into the top of your head. Eventually, a little of it will begin to stick. You should also use acronyms, or "pneumatic devices," to help you memorize.

For example, the prima facie case of a tort action for negligence has several elements: an Act or omission, a Duty, a Breach, Actual cause, Proximate cause, and Damages. The first letters of these elements are A, D, B, A, P, and D. Now, think of a sentence using words beginning with those letters. For example,

*A*nn *D*rop-kicked *B*unnies *A*nd *P*retty *D*uckies. See? You will never forget the elements of negligence again. You can use this technique to remember everything you learn in law school. Employing this method, one student was able to reduce his entire Civil Procedure outline to one word, and finally, to one letter. Then he forgot the letter.

Next, get some of the professor's old exams from the library and try to answer them. As you read them, note that you don't have the foggiest idea what they are asking. You can't even tell what the subject matter of the class was. Put the exams away. This year's test will probably be easier.

Then the two-week exam period begins in earnest, and students begin to feel like a nine-lived cat run over by an eighteen-wheeler. To take their minds off the crush of exams, students engage in a variety of activities, such as:

Trying to concentrate while panicking.
Having anxiety attacks while panicking.
Panicking while panicking.

It is important not to be late to your exams. Your professor might not believe your excuse. The story is told of four Harvard law students who arrived an hour late for their final exam. They explained that they had a flat tire on the way to school, so the professor agreed to give them a makeup exam. Suspecting that the students were lying, the professor placed each student in a separate room and gave each one a copy of the exam. The first question on the exam was: "Which tire?"

I strongly recommend that you type your exams, instead of writing them. There are several advantages to typing. For instance, you can bring a "memory typewriter," and when the exam begins you can push a button and your typewriter will reproduce your entire outline. This is very handy.

You might find it a little difficult to concentrate in the typing room, because all those typewriters pounding together sound like a herd of elephants doing an impersonation of Gregory

Hines. If somebody starts typing before you have even finished reading the first paragraph, don't get upset. It probably means nothing, except that someone is a genius and how are you supposed to compete with a genius and what are you doing in law school anyway!!! Take a deep breath. Take several deep breaths. Now you are hyperventilating and are going to pass out. Cease breathing.

The sound of the typewriters is not the only reason you're having trouble concentrating. You have not slept or eaten for two days. Also, you have not changed your clothes or bathed for a week, and things are beginning to get a little bit itchy. You are wearing a hat to hide the fact that your hair looks like the La Brea tar pits.

Try to hum a tune (to yourself, so that the person next to you doesn't bash you on the head with his typewriter) to help yourself relax. Suddenly—and you have never noticed this before—you realize that *La Bamba* has exactly the same chord progression as *You've Lost That Loving Feeling* and *Twist and Shout*. This will probably be hard to do, but let it go for now. You can think about it later—like during your next exam. Twist a little closer to your typewriter and try to write something quasi-intelligent. Do not shout.

If there is a power failure or your typewriter breaks, don't panic. Calmly remove the paper from the typewriter, gently pick up a pen, and scrawl across the page in ink mixed with blood: "TYPEWRITER BROKE!!!! I WRITE NOW!!!!" Then pass out. To avoid power and equipment failures, you might want to bring in a wheeled cart with about seventeen extra typewriters and a twelve-volt car battery. Better yet, drive a pickup truck full of typewriters into the exam room and open the hood for access to the battery. It would be thoughtful to place a drip pan under the transmission. Also, be sure that the carriage on your typewriter is working, so that you don't end up typing 2,000 letters in one very black spot. This can make your answer hard to read.

The exam questions are usually absolutely hilarious fact situations that just slay students and send them into paroxysms of helpless laughter. The question begins innocently enough with two parties having silly names like "Dan Quaylude" and "Rosanne Barndoor" and ends up in a nuclear explosion stretching halfway across the solar system. The exam asks students to address such realistic issues as whether the Eggshell Skull People who inhabit the planet Pluto are foreseeable plaintiffs. Law professors learn how to write these witty exams at a seminar for new professors, "How to Make Up for Your Humorless Teaching Style on the Final Exam." Try not to let the laughing get out of hand.

While the professor has stressed theory all semester and has insisted that there are no legal rules and that only an idiot would believe that there are rules, the exam tests only on the rules. The rules are printed in heavy black typeface in the commercial outlines, and are therefore called "black letter law." Do not confuse them with black letter theory, which will do you no good whatsoever on the exam.

You should use the "IRAC" method on the exam. "IRAC" stands for Issue, Rule, Application, and Conclusion. Be sure to discuss each part of the formula, except that you can skip the Conclusion, because it doesn't matter which way you come out. Also, there is no time to do the Application, because the exam is so chock-full of issues that you barely have time to list them and to try to state some semblance of a rule using only key words. It shouldn't really be called the "IRAC" method, but "IR" looks kind of stupid and makes it sound like law school exams test only memorization skills. Which, of course, is what they do.

Be sure to confront any ambiguities in the exam. They were probably placed there accidentally, but the professor will never admit this and will insist that they were deliberately placed there for pedagogical purposes (a phrase you hear a lot). For example, suppose Don throws acid at Pat. (Notice that "Don" begins with "D," as does "defendant," and that "Pat" begins with "P," as does "plaintiff." Those professors are geniuses.) The exam doesn't tell you whether the acid made contact—*i.e.*, a harmful or offensive "touching" (what a moronic word)—with Pat. You should confront this ambiguity and write the following:

The facts don't say whether the acid touched Pat. If it did not, it was an assault. If it did, it was a battery. Of course, it was clearly a battery if it was—battery acid!!! (Ha-ha! Get it?)

Professors just love humorous asides like this, and will probably give you several points of extra credit. If they don't, don't blame me. I can't help it if your professor is a prune. Also, to show the professor that you are a nice person, be sure to draw some smiley faces at strategic points throughout your answer.

To promote fairness in grading, law schools have you write an exam number on your exam instead of your name. The story is told of a law school professor whose son was a student in the class. When the professor read the exam answers, he discovered that a third of them began with the words, "Dear Dad."

After the exam, it is generally considered bad form to do "high fives" with members of your study group outside the exam room door. Also, do not review—or "postmortem"—the exam with other students. This is very depressing—especially if you can't even agree on whether it was a torts exam or a contracts exam. On the other hand, if some persistent bozo absolutely INSISTS on reviewing the exam with you, be sure to point out several issues that were NOT on the exam. This will cost him several days' sleep and probably thirty pounds.

To cheer yourself up about exams, you might sing the following song (sung to the tune of the Beach Boys' song *Barbara Ann*):

Chorus
Law law law, law law exam.
Law law law, law.
Oh, law exam, please take my hand, law exam.
You got me rockin' and a rollin',
Rockin' and a reelin',
Law exam, law law, law law exam.

They said, "Be a sport.
Come and learn a tort."
The teacher called my name,
And I went into rigor mort'.

Chorus.

I joined a study group one day.
There's nothing much to say.
I prepared the outline,
But the others got the "A."

Chorus.

On second thought, you might not.

So that you don't get depressed by a low grade in a particular class, the law school waits until *all* your exams are graded before it releases your grades. However, this is small comfort; it's like warming the water before drowning the cat. The day grades come out is a glum day for ninety percent of the students. They have been in the top ten percent all their lives, but now, because of a secret principle of mathematics, only ten percent of them will be in the top ten percent of their law school class. They will immediately blame it all on:

1. The grading system.
2. The professors who failed to explain things.
3. The fact that it was neap tide when they took their exams.

However, amazingly, even if you fixed all these things, STILL only ten percent of the students would be in the top ten percent of their class. No one can explain why.

You look at the sealed envelope containing your grades. Grades are not a matter of life and death, you tell yourself. No. They're a LOT more important than that. You remember how the protagonist in *The Paper Chase* didn't even look at his grade sheet. He made a paper airplane out of it and threw it in the ocean.

What a brave and mature person. *You*, on the other hand, rip the envelope open with bared fangs. Rats. Four F's and a D. The dean calls you into his office and says, "Kid, you've got to stop spending all your time on one subject."

To find some comfort, you open the Bible and read Ezra 9:3. "And when I heard this thing, I rent my garment and my mantle, and plucked off the hair of my head and beard, and sat down astonied." That's exactly how you feel. "Astonied."

CHAPTER 10

The Second and Third Years

The second and third years are about the same as the first year, except that you are a cool second- or third-year student, and now you know that you can make it in law school. Therefore, you live without the sense of terror that was your constant companion during your first year. However, this loss of fear may reduce the students' motivation to do the extra, nonessential things—like read the cases or actually go to class. Some classes look like seminars, with only a handful of students, until the day of the final exam. Then, two hundred students you have never seen before show up, carrying outlines. Astonishingly, half of them will do better on the exam than you will.

To avoid these problems, some professors adopt attendance policies that permit only a few absences. These policies are basically designed to spread communicable diseases throughout the entire class as quickly as possible. Other professors deny non-attending students the right to take the final exam. This avoids the embarrassment of having students who are able to pass the class without the assistance of the professor's brilliant teaching.

You are also much more efficient as an upper-level student.

This efficiency, however, does not result in more free time. Instead, the professors cover the material twice as fast, and now you are required to read a 1,300-page casebook in a single semester instead of a year. This forces you to become a "lean, mean, learning machine"—*i.e.*, you get someone else's outline and memorize it. Of course, this means that you don't develop the critical reasoning skills that law school is supposed to produce. It also means that you cram a forty-page outline into your head the day before the exam, but a week later you can't even remember whether you ever took the class. This approach also produces megapanic attacks from which you will never recover, no matter how long you live. For the rest of your life, you will be plagued by recurrent dreams of taking tests in classes that you have never attended, and you will wake up in a cold sweat. But at least those will be only dreams. For now, the nightmare is real.

One advantage of the second and third years is that you get to choose your teachers (this is called forum shopping) based on the difficulty of their grading curve. The professors believe that you choose their class based on their teaching ability and the centrality of their course to your future career, so it's wisest not to reveal this little trade secret. The professors describe their courses in a list called, appropriately enough, "Course Descriptions." They try to make the courses sound like interesting and important classes that no person who calls herself a lawyer would dare overlook. They do this because if no one attends their class, the dean might fire them. Or worse, make them teach Property.

An honest list of descriptions might look something like this:

Alternative Dispute Resolution (ADR). How people resolve disputes without lawyers, because a simple dogbite case takes five years and $50,000 to get to trial. Learn how to recognize ADR and to squash it.

Conflict of Laws. Memorize several ways of saying, "If you play in my yard, you play by my rules."

Constitutional Law. Ridicule people who still believe that the framers' intent has any relevance whatsoever.

Corporations. How to cheat creditors, shareholders, employ-

ees, consumers, the IRS, and the environment for fun and
profit. Mostly profit.

Criminal Procedure. Learn enough about the rationale behind
the exclusionary rule to defend yourself at cocktail parties.

Evidence. Memorize the hearsay rule and its 50,000 exceptions.
Good for people with a photographic memory and gangs of
free time.

Federal Courts. How to administer prisons, schools, and most of
society from the bench.

Income Taxation. Prepare to be a tax lawyer. A tax lawyer is a
person who is good with numbers but who does not have
enough personality to be an accountant.

Jurisprudence. How to be a jurisprude.

Landlord-Tenant Law. See how medieval English feudal law
has a modern application.

Lawyering Skills. Spend your hard-earned tuition money to
learn what your first employer will pay to teach you anyway.

Products Liability. Set yourself up for life by finding a cockroach
in your Jolt Cola.

Racketeering (RICO). Learn how to use this powerful anti-
extortion law to extort large settlements out of honest business people.[32]

Roman Law. In case you need to sue a Roman.

Securities Regulation. See why Mark Twain said that humans are
the only animals that can be skinned more than once.

State and Local Government. Learn how the broadest govern-
mental powers in America are reserved to a city council
composed of two real estate developers, a retired earthworm
inspector, and a used Styrofoam sales agent.

Wills and Estates. Dead people and their things. Also known as
"Stiffs and their Gifts."

Students think that these classes are difficult, but in reality
they are no harder than an undergraduate chemistry class. In

---

[32] *See* Sedima, S.P.R.L. v. Imrex Co., 473 U.S. 479, 506 (1985) (Marshall, J.,
dissenting).

fact, most of your law professors couldn't even pass a chemistry class today. When they took chemistry years ago, the periodic table only had four elements: earth, air, fire, and water. They learned, for example, that fire has three electrons in the outer shell.

By the third year the students' terror about law school finally dissipates into the atmosphere (and contributes to the hole in the ozone layer). However, the terror is replaced by something equally dreadful: unmitigated boredom. Professors frequently have to summon the paramedics because a student has lost consciousness in class. The only thing that keeps your pulse going is the realization that soon this will be over. Hang in there. To keep your brain from atrophying completely, you could bring a stack of crossword puzzles to class. However, I recommend against raising your hand and interrupting your professor's lecture to ask, "What is a six-letter word for 'catatonic'?"

A lot of people complain about the law school curriculum. They point out that the curriculum has not changed much since the 1870's. That's when Christopher Columbus Langdell at Harvard Law School decided that, with a name like his, he desperately needed to discover something before he died. So he discovered the Socratic method.

Students immediately hated the Socratic method with a passion. Langdell's teaching style was so unpopular that Harvard's law school enrollment plummeted, and rumors circulated that he might be fired. This is true. However, when law professors across the country learned how much students despised the method, they rushed to adopt it, and Langdell's job was spared.

Then, nothing changed for a hundred years. Lawyers may not know much about education, but they know a lot about precedent. Jonathan Swift observed that precedent is important because, in the law, anything that has been done before may legally be done again. So the Socratic method continued its reign.

The Socratic method is good for teaching students how to "think like a lawyer." However, because it's so slow, it's not much good for teaching anything else. Consequently, legal education emphasizes legal reasoning skills over specific areas of the law. This generalist approach, of course, has deficiencies. For example, in recent years law practice has become increasingly complex and specialized. In the old days most lawyers were sole practitioners, and they had to do everything from defending dogbites to negotiating corporate mergers with space aliens. A lawyer with a formbook and a Dictaphone was an instant expert in anything.

Nowadays things are different. There are megafirms, each with a huge flock (technically, a "pride") of lawyers.[33] Each lawyer focuses on one narrow subspecialty—for example, how to convert backyard birdhouses into time-share resort condominiums.

There is also much more law than there used to be. Sometime after the 1870's the New Deal occurred, accompanied by the rise of the regulatory state. In the old days you could clear a wilderness, settle a territory, and declare a war without ever thinking about lawyers. Today you have to consult a lawyer before you hose out the grease pan in your garage. Preferably a grease pan specialist.

In addition, some of the cases studied in law school are out of date. You read hoary medieval cases in which Sir Gawain attacked Baron Relic. Studying ancient swordfights may be interesting, but it leaves you unprepared to deal with the modern world of electronic fund transfers and computer software licensing agreements. Another problem is that you can learn the basic analytical skills in your first year. You endure the second year patiently enough, mostly because you're being wined and dined by prospective employers. Also, there is some satisfaction in being an upperclass student and lording it over the first-years. However, by the time you're in your third year, you are bored out of your mind. Of course, the dry professors don't help. W. H. Auden defined a professor as a person who talks in someone else's sleep.

One difficulty with the upper-level curriculum is that, basically, there is no upper-level curriculum. There is merely a smorgasbord of unrelated courses. Students experiencing indigestion

---

[33] Or a "glut." *Cf.* a hoard of doctors, or an evasion of administrators.

from combining the enchiladas of environmental law with the fishsticks of federal taxation are desperately reaching for the antacid of reform. To coin a phrase.

Consequently, recently law schools have begun talking about curriculum reform. Of course, any lawyer can TALK. Lawyers earn their bread by the sweat of their tongue. The astonishing thing is that a few law schools are actually doing something about it.

One curriculum reform is to provide more training in lawyering skills, such as drafting documents and trying cases. Some schools have adopted this reform because employers have complained, with mosquito-like persistence, that new law graduates can't find the courthouse door, even when they are dropped off on the front steps.

However, law professors don't particularly like to teach lawyering skills. If professors had enjoyed the practical aspects of lawyering, they wouldn't have given up a salary of a zillion dollars a year in law practice. Being forced to teach those things without earning a lawyer's salary is the worst of all possible worlds.

The other major curriculum reform is specialization. Rather than take a lot of survey courses in areas you are not interested in, you can concentrate in a particular area of the law, much like having an undergraduate major. Some schools are beginning to offer specialties in such areas as environmental law, intellectual property, health care law, litigation, and international law. You can receive a certificate stating that you've specialized in a particular area, which can help set you apart when you look for jobs. It also pleases clients, who, oddly enough, don't like paying for a new lawyer's on-the-job training.

Some law professors object, because reforming the curriculum is a lot of work. "We only finished reforming the curriculum a hundred years ago," they complain, "and you're already talking about doing it AGAIN?" Then they go back to sleep.

Other professors object that some students don't know what specialty to choose. Therefore, quite logically, NOBODY should be allowed to choose. Some argue that students might want (or be forced) to change specialties after entering law practice, in which case their handsome specialization certificate will be suitable for conversion into a handsome paper airplane. Learning a new area without taking the professor's introductory course is, you understand, unthinkable. Someone might even have to read a book, or something equally odious. Students should be able to stop learning when they graduate, just as the professors did.

So when it comes to curriculum reform, most law schools are still at the talking stage. This is the stage where law professors feel most comfortable. They may not know much about pedagogy, but they know a lot about parliamentary procedure and seating arrangements. So far, most law faculties are still discussing the motion to table the motion to move the table. Meanwhile, don't hold your breath.

11

Law Review and Other Cocurricular Programs

Being fully committed to providing the best possible educational opportunities for every student, law schools offer cocurricular programs, like law journals and moot court. Then, quite naturally, they let hardly anyone participate in them.

The most elitist organization is the law review, which is generally restricted to the top ten percent of the class. These students are given this special honor so that employers will not overlook them just because they are at the top of their class. Law review editors spend their time doing meaningful educational tasks like checking the citation form of articles they don't understand. Law review editors are the big snots around the school.[34]

However, law review editors may be the biggest dupes of all. Consider this passage from a well known American novel:

Saturday morning was come, and all the summer world was bright and fresh, and brimming with life. There was a song in

---

[34] Question: How many law review editors does it take to screw in a light bulb? Answer: Only one. He sits still and the world revolves around him.

every heart; and if the heart was young the music issued at the lips. There was cheer in every face and a spring in every step. The locust trees were in bloom and the fragrance of the blossoms filled the air. Cardiff Hill, beyond the village and above it, was green with vegetation; and it lay just far enough away to seem a Delectable Land, dreamy, reposeful, and inviting.

Tom appeared on the sidewalk with a bucket of whitewash and a long-handled brush. He surveyed the fence, and all gladness left him and a deep melancholy settled down upon his spirit. Thirty yards of board fence nine feet high. Life to him seemed hollow, and existence but a burden. Sighing he dipped his brush and passed it along the topmost plank; repeated the operation; did it again; compared the insignificant whitewashed streak with the far-reaching continent of unwhitewashed fence, and sat down on a tree-box, discouraged.[35]

You know the story. Through a brilliant use of reverse psychology, Tom Sawyer was able to hoodwink his gullible friends into thinking that it was actually a *privilege* to whitewash the fence. They did all the work for nothing; in fact, they even paid him for the privilege.

The modern analogue to Tom's whitewash is, of course, law review. Law schools want to have law reviews. However, hiring people to write, edit, and cite-check is expensive. Under standard university wage scales, buying one hundred hours of this kind of skilled labor can cost nearly one hundred dollars. So law schools get students to do it for free, and they even get some of the best students to do it. All they have to do is *limit* the opportunity to the top students, and busy law students line up like Tom Sawyer's friends, begging for the opportunity to spend countless grueling unpaid hours working on the law review.

Law students, however, are not the only ones hoodwinked: law professors across the country spend much of their professional lives slaving away on articles that they will publish *for free*. "It's an honor," their deans tell them. "A privilege. You're lucky that the law reviews don't charge *you* money for publishing your

---

[35] Mark Twain, *The Adventures of Tom Sawyer* 26–27 (1876).

articles." Then the deans secretly call each other on the telephone and laugh until the tears stream down their faces.

The law review experience begins with the selection process. Membership is determined by exam grades, based on the theory that short-term memory is clearly the best measure of student intelligence. A few students are given permission to write on to law review, in a grudging admission that writing ability might possibly somehow someday have some tangential relevance to editing. So write-on students spend all their waking hours for weeks or months writing and editing an article in order to have the privilege of doing more writing and editing. Write-on competitions have therefore been compared to a pie-eating contest in which the first prize is another pie.

In any event, law review membership develops extremely valuable legal skills. For example, students become intimately familiar with the *Bluebook*. This is a definite benefit, assuming that you consider it a benefit to have an intimate familiarity with mass psychosis. Law review editors also, by definition, edit. The brightest person on the law review is given the position of Split Infinitive Editor.

But not all of the law review experience is *Bluebook*ing and editing. Law review members are also expected to write notes

and comments. These pieces typically have strict page limitations, mostly because there are limits on how big of a fool one can
make of oneself in fifteen pages. However, some people seem to
have a special talent for overcoming even this obstacle. This is
the reason that notes and comments used to be anonymous.
Anonymity of authorship could be an advantage for professors,
too, as the Robert Bork hearings showed.

Law review editors also get to evaluate articles written by law
professors. Of course, these articles are not about the LAW.
Nowadays law professors consider articles about legal doctrine to
be pedestrian.[36] An article like that might actually make a real
difference in someone's life, and law professors have no time for
pursuits as mundane as that. They are too busy writing articles
about meta-law: the philosophical, political, sociological, and lin-
guistic aspects of law.

For example, some law review articles deal with law and social
science. These articles are based on sociological studies that
show, for example, that business people usually do not pay the
slightest attention to contract law,[37] and that the only people in
the entire world who have any idea of contract law are first-year
law students. Another study shows that medical malpractice reforms have made no measurable difference in liability insurance
costs.[38] Naturally, people who have devoted their entire lives to
these subjects find these studies distressing, to say the least. So
unless you like having enemies, it is better not to burst their
theoretical bubbles by revealing the law's (lack of) impact in the
real world.

If law review makes you work your brain to the bone, you
should expect the camaraderie and friendship on law review to
make up for it. Unfortunately, the only positive thing one can say
about being with other law review members is that it is more fun

---

[36] Or possibly, if the articles are about horse law, equestrian.

[37] Stewart MacAuley, *Non-Contractual Relations in Business: A Preliminary Study*,
28 Am. Soc. Rev. 55 (1963).

[38] Frank A. Sloan, *State Responses to the Malpractice Insurance "Crisis" of the 1970s:
An Empirical Assessment*, 9 J. Health Politics, Policy & Law 692 (1984).

than being with the faculty. Of course, lots of things meet that standard, including going down to the gas station and jumping on the ding hose. However, the prospect of being part of a close community of bright and dedicated young scholars does have some romantic utopian appeal. Regrettably, when you get on the law review you learn that it is about as communitarian as the United States Marine Corps. The only reason that some law reviews have dispensed with cattle prods and flogging is that state law schools are subject to the cruel and unusual punishment clause of the Eighth Amendment. However, the Federalist Society is currently working on that problem.

Some law schools have law journals in addition to the law review. These journals usually focus on a specific area of the law, and have names like *The Journal of Comparative Funeral Law*, or *The Review of International Agreements Governing Intestinal Tapeworms* (*Northern Hemisphere*). They concentrate in a particular area so that they don't have to be named *The Second-String Law Review*, which they would consider somewhat demeaning.

Another type of cocurricular program is upper-level moot court. These students are the ones with bared fangs and fire in their eyes, who can't wait to get out of school and litigate the living corpuscles out of every warm-blooded creature. So they start doing it in law school. They learn the basic rules of advocacy, such as:

If the law is against you, hit the facts.
If the facts are against you, hit the law.
If the law and the facts are against you, hit the table.

They also get to go to competitions in distant places, like Eyesocket, Nevada. Compared to attending law school classes, this is pretty exciting.

There are also student organizations. Some of these ostensibly focus on a particular topic or interest, like "The Coalition for the Legal Empowerment of Undersea Protozoa," or "Future Trial Attorneys for the Clinically Brain Dead." However, they really exist only to provide résumé padding. A student wants to be able to say that he is the Exalted Grand Excellent Potentate of the Ancient Royal Order of Backbenchers. This is supposed to impress employers.

Other student organizations, like legal fraternities, don't make any such pretense. They openly admit that they exist to advance people's careers. They put up posters showing that five of the sitting Supreme Court justices (a working majority) belong to Beta Grabba Fee. The posters also include testimonials from lawyers basically saying that it's *who* you know that counts, and that if they had not belonged to that particular fraternity, their careers would have been in the Dumpster. So give us your sixty bucks. These organizations perceive no need to have an independent reason for existing, since fear and greed can legitimately stand on their own.

Another organization, called the Federalist Society, has appeared at some American law schools. The Federalist Society essentially believes that things were a whole lot better in 1791 than they are today, and the sooner we return to that golden age when states were unencumbered by the Bill of Rights, the better. Their organizational efforts have been impeded, however, by the fact that Federalist membership dues must be paid in gold coins, since the society refuses to recognize paper money as legal tender.

12

My Theory Is Bigger Than Your Theory[39]

If it hasn't happened already, during your second or third year you will be exposed to some relatively new schools of thought. Although these schools of thought are a little unusual, they are not to be rejected out of hand. They are to be carefully considered and weighed. And then rejected.

One current trend is the law and literature movement, which applies methods of literary analysis to legal texts and examines the treatment of legal issues in literature. I have some difficulty with this area, since frankly I don't understand literature very well. I think that a literary work can usually be reduced to a single sentence that captures its essence. A few examples come to mind:

Odyssey: Never underestimate the value of a good travel agent.
War and Peace: Russian winters are darn cold.
Richard III: Never vote for anybody named Richard.
King Lear: How sharper than a thankful child, to have a tooth-less serpent (or something like that).
Metamorphosis: Being a bug is a drag.

---

[39] *See* Gary Peller, *Reason and the Mob: The Politics of Representation*, Tikkun, July/Aug. 1987, at 28, 29.

Some law and literature groupies try to apply methods of literary criticism to the law. This approach, however, has limitations. Since *literature* is supposed to make the reader *feel* things, some literary critics say that the reader's meaning is as important as the author's. *Law*, on the other hand, describes the official decisions of government, and so the subjective meaning of an individual reader (as opposed to the objective meaning to the average citizen) is irrelevant—at least to the government. It does no good for a burglar to argue, "To me, the burglary statute is really a statement about how we intrude in each other's lives, and nothing more." The court, perceiving that there is in fact something more, will probably respond to the defendant's argument with a little intrusiveness of its own.

A second movement is called Critical Legal Studies (CLS). Critical Legal Studies rests on the following irrefutable syllogism:

Major Premise: Lots of cases could be decided either way.
Minor Premise: I don't like the way a lot of cases have been decided.
Conclusion: The law is a crock.
Practical Application: Come the revolution.

When you ask what happens after the revolution, it gets really fuzzy. Apparently, "hegemony," "illegitimate hierarchies," and other multisyllabic evils will be replaced by "communities of life" with "negative capability," "role jumbling," and "a constitutionalism of permanent mobilization," which will permit us to develop the "species nature," realize "concrete universality," and "discover the organic unity of each other's personalities."[40] Don't worry too much about the specifics. After the revolution is over, Central Command, assisted by the Rev-

---

[40] *See generally* Roberto Unger, *Knowledge and Politics* (1975); Roberto Unger, *False Necessity: Anti-Necessitarian Social Theory in the Service of Radical Democracy. Part I of Politics, A Work in Constructive Social Theory* (1987).

olutionary Army, will persuasively explain the details to the survivors.

"Crits" don't believe in hierarchy. These are people who graduated in the top ten percent of their class, were on the law review, are full professors at the nation's elite law schools, and spend their lives training people for a monopolistic profession in a country that owes much of its standard of living to the fact that it keeps most of the world's population out. Well, except for *that*, they don't believe in hierarchy.

Some Crits argue that, to eliminate illegitimate hierarchies, all jobs should be rotated. I am not kidding. So try this. Ask your CLS professor how come he hasn't, even once, let the building custodian teach his class while the professor scrubs out the toilets in the third-floor bathroom. Huh? How come? He'll tell you to get the hey out of his office, and to take your hegemonic positivist thinking with you. Suddenly, it dawns on you that in the Crits' postrevolutionary world, some people will be wielding the levers of power and others will be wielding the scrub brushes. Apparently, there are illegitimate hierarchies and legitimate ones. If you know what I mean.

Crits say that all language and all truth are indeterminate. But if truth really is indeterminate, why do Crits so fiercely insist that their own view is correct? Why should a person even bother to *have* a view?

Crits believe that all law is politics, and they spend their time "trashing" or "unmasking" the law to reveal its underlying value preferences. The revelation that the law actually protects real human values has been so shocking as to produce a crisis of confidence in the law as an institution. Previously, everyone thought that the law simply existed for its own sake, much like the Vice Presidency. But Crits argue that the law is hypocritical, and they deconstruct it to expose the hidden values it refuses to acknowledge. Then, after taking us into the wilderness and leaving us there,[41] they zoom off in their BMW's

---

[41] Someone said that the legal realists did this, too, but I don't remember who said it. In any event, the wilderness is getting pretty crowded.

to continue their class struggle against hierarchy and privilege.[42]

Crits talk funny. One famous CLS article[43] sounds like "a pair of old acid-heads chewing over a passage in Sartre."[44] An example:

> It is not inconsistent to, on the one hand, realize the projective temporal character of human existence, in which no one is identity, and the living subject is continually not what he or she is by moving into the next moment in a creative and constitutive way.[45]

Crits also talk a lot about "intersubjective zap" and "unalienated relatedness."[46] They speak in this manner because if they just openly announced that, what the hey, we should overthrow American democracy and replace it with a Marxist utopia,[47] people would begin wondering why the only Marxists left in the entire world teach at American universities. The Crits' strategy has worked pretty well, considering that they have been able to last two decades on about ten minutes' worth of ideas.

Another school of thought is called "law and economics." While Crits believe that all law is aimed at SUPPORTING free-market capitalism, the "Econs" believe that all law is an unwar-

---

[42] *See* M.H. Hoeflich, *Introduction, Symposium: After the War: Poverty Law in the 1980s*, 38 Emory L.J. 565, 566 (1989).

[43] Peter Gabel & Duncan Kennedy, *Roll Over Beethoven*, 36 Stan. L. Rev. 1 (1984).

[44] David Luban, *Legal Modernism*, 84 Mich. L. Rev. 1656, 1671 (1986).

[45] Gabel & Kennedy, *supra* note 43, at 19.

[46] Crits argue that all power structures, including language, are propped up from the inside, perpetuate hierarchy, and exclude others. Therefore, Crits use an untranslatable, circular, self-referential vocabulary that supports their arguments from the inside, perpetuates the hierarchy of the Crits as Gnostics who pretend to know a Mystery, and excludes others. *See* Orson Scott Card, *Prophets and Assimilationists*, 13 Sunstone 39 (Feb. 1989).

[47] Since Crits are radical nondeterminists, they quite naturally advocate one of the most deterministic political ideologies ever created: Marxism.

ranted INTERFERENCE with free-market capitalism. Other than that, the two groups pretty much see eye to eye.

Econs basically believe that material wealth is the highest human value, and that justice, fairness, the environment, and protecting the helpless all cost money, and are therefore "economically inefficient." The money could be better spent on much more transcendent things, like pet rocks, hemorrhoid pads, and other items needed to satisfy AGGREGATE DEMAND.

Econs prove their theories by devising little mathematical formulas that assume whole truckloads of untrue things[48] and then come to a particular conclusion. The conclusion is always—get this—"The market will take care of it itself." SURPRISE!!! According to the Econs, there is a GIANT INVISIBLE DIS-EMBODIED HAND that magically takes care of everything. Before you get too excited about this, remember that this is the same invisible hand that gave us the invisible GREAT DE-PRESSION. Oh. THAT invisible hand.

When you point out that the assumptions in the formulas are simplistic (a euphemism for "false"), the Econs get really testy and tell you that you don't understand the discipline.[49] Be-sides, although sitting in an office and writing little mathematical formulas may not be the most EFFECTIVE way to solve the world's problems, it is at least one of the highest paid, and you can't have everything. Moreover, law and economics doesn't require any empirical studies, which, after all, would be tedious and time-consuming. So the Econs don't want to hear you say that their delicate theories are about to be smashed flat by a ton of hard facts. Also, they have no time to

---

[48] The character of the assumptions is illustrated by the story of an economics professor who was walking across campus with a student. "Look," said the student, pointing at the ground, "a five-dollar bill." "It can't be," responded the professor. "If it were there, somebody would have picked it up by now." Judy Jones & William Wilson, *An Incomplete Education* 125 (1987).

[49] "Economics is a closed system; internally it is perfectly logical, operating according to a consistent set of principles. Unfortunately, the same could be said of psychosis." *Id.* at 124.

listen to you, as they are busy trying to get the math section back on the LSAT.

Econs believe that modern judges should analyze and resolve all legal issues by using the tools of law and economics. The whole evolution of the common law, they urge, is to get judges to walk upright as *Homo economicus*.

Let me give you an example of law and economics. Suppose Seller has signed a contract to sell widgets to Buyer. Then Third Party comes and offers Seller one dollar more than the contract price. Many Econs believe—now listen closely—that Seller has a MORAL OBLIGATION to breach his solemn contract with Buyer and pay damages so that the widgets will go to their highest and best use. Econs call this greedy and wretched act of treachery an EFFICIENT BREACH. Never mind that Buyer has to scramble to find other widgets. Never mind that BUYER should have the opportunity to sell the widgets to Third Party and get the profits, instead of that breaching grimeball Seller. Never mind that the certainty and stability of contracts will be undermined, resulting in fewer contracts and ultimately less economic exchange. Although Econs admit that this free-for-all law-of-the-jungle auction-without-a-gavel may be unjust, justice is mere chickenspit compared to wealth. While money may not buy happiness, it at least affords us the particular kind of misery that we most enjoy.

So the Crits attack from the left and the Econs from the right. The Crits are negative and the Econs are positive. Wouldn't it be fun to put all the Crits and Econs in the same room and see whether, like ions, they combine to form one humongous molecule of inert gas? Unfortunately, since most of these people refuse to get in the same room with each other, modern science will never know whether it would work.

CHAPTER
13

Interviewing for Jobs

It used to be that at the beginning of their second year, students would participate in on-campus interviews for employment nearly two years later. However, it was quickly recognized that this was not nearly early enough. So, job interviews now begin in the students' FIRST year, nearly THREE years before they graduate. The students work for the law firms the following summer and have a dandy time being escorted around to fancy restaurants and on trips down the Colorado River. Of course, as much as the students appreciate these flattering jaunts, they can't help noticing that they never meet any lawyers who actually work for the firm in any of these places (other than those who are chaperoning the law students).

Law firms tell a joke about someone who visits heaven and hell. In heaven people are playing boring harps. In hell they are having a wonderful time at a terrific party. The person therefore decides to go to hell after he dies. However, when he arrives, he sees that the people there are all being roasted on spits or are slaving away in the mines. When he asks what happened to the party, the Devil replies, "Oh, that was our summer clerkship program." Law firms don't tell this joke to the clerks.

Before you interview, you will need to prepare a "résumé." It is also called a "curriculum vitae," a Latin phrase meaning "preposterous fable." There is a fine art to interpreting résumés. "Top 10%" means "top 20%." "Top 20%" means "top half." "Middle of the class" means "bottom half." Law schools get extremely angry when students pad their résumés like this. They give moralistic lectures telling students that it is just plain dishonest. Because they are the nation's leading law schools, the twenty-five schools in the Top Ten get particularly huffy about it. One final suggestion: to avoid annoying federal interference, take care not to send your résumé through the mails.

The students give their résumés to the Placement Office and tell it which employers they are interested in. The Placement Office forwards the résumés to the designated employers, who then decide which students they would like to interview on campus. However, a few law schools do not let the employers screen the résumés and interview only those students they are really interested in. Instead, students sign up for interviews, and a computer randomly narrows the sign-up list to the number of interview time slots. This random selection method has the advantage of being completely fair to all parties, since it wastes everyone's time equally.

At most schools, though, the Placement Office publishes the list of students that a given employer wants to interview. However, merely appearing on the list is not nearly enough recognition to satisfy some students. So they also proudly display their green "interview slips" in their front shirt pocket. Students strut around like peacocks, competing to be the person with the most ostentatious display of color. (Later, they will compete to be the person who wears a suit on the most days.) In case someone misses the visual message, several times a minute students will mention the names of the firms they're interviewing with, as in:

YOU: It sure is a beautiful day.
CLASSMATE: Yes, especially because today I'm interviewing with Blah, Blah & Blah.
YOU: It's very warm outside.
CLASSMATE: Yes. I shouldn't have worn my wool suit, but Blah, Blah & Blah is a very elite firm.

YOU: I hope I have enough money to pay my rent this month.
CLASSMATE: Did I mention that the starting salary at Blah,
    Blah & Blah is $75,000 a year? Plus the bonus, of course.
YOU: If you don't shut up, I'm going to give you a bonus you'll
    never forget—and it's nontaxable, nontransferable, and non-
    refundable. So stuff it.

Then you interview with the employers on campus. However,
people realize that it is impossible in one twenty-minute interview to learn enough about a firm to decide whether you want to
trust to its care your career training, your professional reputation,
and the financial security of you and your family, not to mention
half your waking hours for the rest of your entire life. Doing that
takes at least two or three twenty-minute interviews. For this
reason, law firms invite you to make a "call-back," a "flyout," or
a "dogsled-ride-back," depending on where they are located.
Whatever they call it, you get to spend a day at the firm and learn
all there is to know. Watch for subtle signs of discontent among
the attorneys. For example, pay special attention if an associate
at the firm runs past you down the hall screaming. This is generally not a good sign.

You should ask how many hours associates are required to bill.
In some big firms associates bill as many as 3,000 hours a year.
One student asked if the associates ever do anything fun to-

gether. "Sure," the interviewer replied. "About ten o'clock we knock off for an hour and go play a game of racquetball." The student observed, "What a great way to break up the morning." The interviewer responded, "Morning?"

Lawyers are defined as "professional employees" and are therefore exempt from the federal labor laws, which set forth the minimum standards of human decency. If during your visit to the restroom you see cots and complete changes of clothing, this is a bad sign. It is an especially bad sign if the law firm is having its offices rezoned as "residential." So all in all, the big firm scene might not be for you. Particularly if they don't make you an offer.

And they won't. This is because the students at the top of the class were not satisfied by having their names printed on the interview lists, by displaying their green interviewing cards in their shirt pocket, by wearing a suit every single day during interviewing season, by mentioning their interviews in gloating tones at every possible opportunity, and by comparing their outrageous starting salaries. No, these young egos need more. So these students hoard all the offers they receive. Even though they can only accept one of their many offers, they will not even consider rejecting a single offer until after the interviewing season is over. They want to savor their sweet success as long as possible. Meanwhile, the rest of the students can pound sand.

However, you should not get discouraged if a big firm does not make you an offer. You should remember that there are many job opportunities and lots of different types of work that lawyers do. For example:

Corporate Work: drafting documents for scumsucking corporations that poison huge numbers of innocent people.

Litigation: defending scumsucking corporations that poison huge numbers of innocent people.

Criminal Defense: defending scumsucking individuals who poison a few innocent people at a time, mostly because they lack the capital and technology to poison huge numbers of innocent people.

Public Interest Work: suing scumsucking corporations that poison huge numbers of innocent people. Earning less than what the law firms on the other side of the litigation pay their pencil sharpeners.

So that should make you feel better. Weigh your options carefully.

If you want to delay making a choice, or if you want to wean yourself from poverty slowly, you might do a judicial clerkship for a year. This is an opportunity to hone your skills polishing the shoes and ironing the robes of some political hack with life tenure. You might get to clerk for an "associate justice" of the U.S. Supreme Court, or maybe even a "full" justice. If so, you get to write constitutional decisions that dramatically change the entire structure of Western civilization (drawing broadly on your vast experience as a law student and your undergraduate degree in sports medicine), while your justice whiles away the time sharpening the teeth of his prize pit bull with a chainsaw, or whittling the heads off dolls. Also, you get to write repeatedly the two words most commonly used by Supreme Court justices: "Habeas denied."

CHAPTER 14

Making Your Getaway

Before you graduate, when you have almost completed law school, you take a test called the "Professional Responsibility Exam." This test asks you questions about ethics and morality. If your answers reveal that you have the slightest trace of a conscience remaining, you are scheduled for surgery. During the surgery they remove the particular lobe of the brain that is causing the problem. Although this procedure may seem harsh, you should be very grateful. Without it you would be completely incapable of functioning as a normal lawyer. Perhaps you have noticed that many young lawyers wear sporty sweatbands on their heads when they play racquetball. They do this to hide the scar.

Before you take the bar and become a full-fledged lawyer, you must do one more thing. You need to ask your law school dean to write a letter recommending you for admission to the bar. The dean's time is very limited, since he teaches a full three hours out of a forty-hour week.

There is an old story about what it's like to be a dean. The outgoing dean explains to the new dean that, if trouble arises, sage advice is contained in three envelopes in the desk. A year later a serious problem arises. The dean opens the first envelope. The note says, "Stall." The dean does, and the problem eventually goes away. A year later another serious problem arises. The dean opens the second envelope. The note says, "Appoint a committee." The dean does, and the committee solves the problem. A year later the worst problem of all arises. The dean can't see how he can possibly solve it. He opens the third envelope. The note says, "Make three envelopes."

Once a high school principal asked a university president to supply a graduation speaker. The principal made it clear that he wanted "nothing lower than a dean." The university president responded, "Sir, there *is* nothing lower than a dean."

Since he is so busy, your dean will probably send a recommendation letter that looks like this:

Dear Sir or Madam:

I have been asked to write a letter recommending _____ for admission to the state bar. Since I write a lot of these letters, I trust you will not object to the format below. I have checked the appropriate blanks. In my judgment, this person:

Integrity
____ Is as pure as mountain springwater.
____ Is as pure as mountain springwater 100 miles downstream.
____ Are you familiar with feedlot runoff?

Intelligence
____ Is as brilliant as Einstein, but has a better hairdresser.
____ Meets the implied warranty of merchantability: is fit for the ordinary purposes for which lawyers are used.
____ Received an F-minus in my class. Giving this person an F would have distorted the grading curve beyond the range of current mathematical theory.

Knowledge
____ Understands the Rule Against Perpetuities, and has explained it to me several times.
____ Knows what "unalienated relatedness" means.
____ Realizes now that no other success can compensate for being a total failure.

Aspirations

____ Desires world peace, equal justice, and an end to hunger and poverty. Also wants a private jet and a vacation home in Switzerland.

Therefore, I do ____ do not ____ recommend this person for admission to the state bar.

Sincerely,

Filbert Q. Oxbreath IV
Dean and Grand Pooh-Bah

Since your dean took the time from his crushing schedule to write this letter for you, he must not be such a bad person after all. In fact, from now on he will make you one of his personal pen pals. Even though he didn't have two seconds for you in law school, you will suddenly become his close, first-name-basis, bosom buddy forever. Throughout your entire mortal existence, no matter where your career takes you, through all the ups and

downs of life, your dean will regularly write you thoughtful and personally computer-generated letters—asking you for money. You just can't put a price on a friendship like that. *He*, however, does have a ballpark figure in mind.

Finally graduation day comes. You and your classmates put on medieval black robes and balance what appear to be square fris-bees on your heads. You march regally in front of a throng of proud and (after paying tuition for three years) impecunious spouses, parents, jealous siblings, small children, and household pets. You then listen to a couple of hours of stirring exhortations to be ethical and give service throughout your life. By now, of course, this is deeply ingrained in your psyche, since you heard it all once before, three years ago, on the first day of law school.

By law, all graduation speakers are required to use certain phrases in their speech. It's most efficient if they're combined in one sentence, like: "You, the rising generation, stand at the crossroads ["threshold" is equally acceptable in some states], poised for flight into the great unknown, with the past as pro-logue, with the future in your hands, and with the hope of Amer-ica upon you." Naturally, any reference in these speeches to earning a living is strictly forbidden.

You might enjoy these talks, if it weren't for the fact that you're sitting in the direct sunlight in a robe made of thermal-insulated black cloth. You are beginning to smell like a baked potato.

You reflect back upon the three years of law school: the time spent as a terrified first-year student trying not to flunk out, as a terrified second-year student trying to find a summer clerkship, and as a terrified third-year student trying to find a job. Oh, those halcyon days! They say that life never gets better than this.

Then the dean gives some awards to a few smarty-pants know-it-all students who, you can just tell, are way too intellectual to ever be successful practitioners. Lastly, the dean begins reading the names of the graduates. He correctly pronounces the name of Michael Brown-Momrath-Outgrabe-Okefenokee-Endoplasmic-Reticulum-Stratford-on-Avon, Jr. Of course, he mispronounces your name. But it's over, and you're thrilled. You leave law school with mixed emotions: joy and rapture.

CHAPTER
15

The Bar Exam

After you have graduated, you have to go through an initiation rite similar to those of certain college fraternities and sororities. Initiates to those groups get off easy, however, since they only have to eat live chickens and stuff goldfish up their noses, whereas you have to go through eight weeks of preparing for and taking the bar exam. The state bar association says that bar exams are designed to ensure the competency of the practicing bar. You learned about them in your antitrust class, under the topic of "Market Entry Barriers." They make it possible for people who are already admitted to the bar to make a living wage (*i.e.*, about $200,000 a year). You will probably feel somewhat better about the exam's rationale after you pass it.

You will need to take an intensive seven-week course, costing a drillion dollars, to prepare for the bar exam. Wait a minute, you say. Why did I borrow ten drillion dollars (exceeding the national debt of some Third World countries) and spend three years of my life going to law school? Didn't law school teach me the law? No, you idiot. Law school's purpose is not to teach you the *law*. Law school taught you to THINK LIKE A LAWYER, unless you attended one of the elite schools, and then it taught you to think like a medieval philosopher, or a business school dropout. So you have to take the bar prep course.

Since it's an almost impossible task to memorize three years of material for one exam, bar prep courses use three principal techniques:

1. A tape recorder under your pillow as you sleep.
2. Mass hypnosis.
3. Blood doping.

Students for whom these techniques do not work are actually driven, as a last resort, to study the huge pile of outlines prepared by the bar prep course.

When you apply to take the bar exam, you must provide the names of 500 character witnesses. For obvious reasons, practicing lawyers may not be used as character witnesses. You must also list the exact address of every place you've ever lived since you were born. Heaven help you if your parents were in the military, or if you don't have a photographic memory.

Each state writes its own bar exam, which is an enormous duplication of effort and which produces bar exams of widely varying quality and difficulty. The exams in some large states, like New York and California, are very difficult to pass on the first attempt. Not long ago someone passed the California bar exam on his twenty-seventh attempt. He was the only person admitted in California that year. On the other hand, bar exams in less populous states are typically much easier. In some states, the only requirement for passing the bar exam is that you spell your first name correctly.

It would be much simpler if a group of skilled professionals wrote one bar exam that all fifty states could use, just as occurs with certified public accountant exams and securities licensing exams. In fact, a group of skilled professionals *does* write nation-wide bar exam questions. The National Conference of Bar Examiners writes a set of multiple-choice questions called the Multistate Bar Exam, which most states use. It also writes excellent essay questions, but most states insist on using their homegrown products instead. If you ask why, the state bar will tell you that each state needs to test for competency on *that state's*

law. But in fact, all bar exams test primarily on *general American law*, with only a few local issues thrown in.

Still, the bar examiners insist that those few local issues are important. But then they can't explain why, if a student achieves a high enough score on the Multistate Bar Exam, the examiners don't even bother to read the student's essays, which include the sprinkling of local issues. The truth is that they *do* believe that a knowledge of general American law is enough.

The primary *advantage* of a national bar exam, from your perspective, is that you wouldn't have to take a new bar exam if you wanted to practice in another state. The primary *disadvantage* of a national bar exam, from the bar examiners' perspective, is that you wouldn't have to take a new bar exam if you wanted to practice in another state. So at least everyone sees the same issue clearly.

Meanwhile, for all you indignant bar examiners who want to write me threatening letters, think about it this way: the more people who read this book, the fewer who will become lawyers. So what are you complaining about?

CHAPTER
16

The First Year of
Law Practice

Well, you finally got a job at the law firm of Driftwood, Flotsam & Jetsam, and you're ready to begin practicing law. Unfortunately, the first year of law practice feels like the first year of law school all over again. Everything is new, and the learning curve is a vertical line that stretches straight into the clouds. Goethe spoke the truth: "Nothing is more terrible than to see ignorance in action." You discover all the things that law school *failed* to teach you—like what lawyers really do every day. These things include:

Sitting at your desk while meeting with clients.
Sitting at your desk while meeting with other lawyers.
Sitting at your desk while drafting documents.
Sitting in the library while doing research.
Going to lunch and eating heavy restaurant food.
Going back to the office and sitting around some more.
Wondering why in the world you're getting so flabby.

While your body is getting softer, your mind and heart are hardening into frozen steel. You learn the lawyerly arts of denying compensation to worthy victims and of foreclosing on orphans. Yes, you are becoming a professional. This is the life you have dreamed of.

You are constantly aware of the tyranny of the time sheet. The firm has you keep track of your billable time in milliseconds. It divides time up into such small segments because you are constantly being interrupted, and on average you have to change gears about forty-seven times per second. Be sure to bill it all.

When you go to lunch, bring some clients along so you can bill the entire lunch hour to them. An accurate billing statement for the hour would read:

Reviewing menu .1 hour; conference with waiter re today's specials .1 hour; visiting salad bar (including travel time both ways) .2 hour; eating salad .1 hour; peeling artichoke .1 hour; eating fettuccine Alfredo .2 hour; conference with clients re whether to order any dessert today .1 hour; legal advice .1 hour. Total 1.0 hour.

You will also bill the cost of the lunch to the clients. Lawyers NEVER pay overhead. They bill the costs of all photocopies, faxes, and postage to their clients. If they could, lawyers would bill their electric bill directly to their clients. But they can't. So they don't pay their electric bill.

After lunch you go back to the office and try to stay awake—which is always difficult, given the nature of your work. To make matters worse, the fettuccine Alfredo is causing you to go into pasta shock, a condition in which all the blood drains from your brain to try to digest the glop of paste in your stomach. In the future you will have to skip lunch.

But there is one upside to law practice. After all these years of sacrifice and poverty, you FINALLY have an income. And not only an income, but a BIG income. In your first year of practice you are making more money than your law professors. HA! So there is justice, after all.

Well, what should you spend the money on? You *could* pay off your staggering student loans. No, leave that until after you

retire. Right now it's time to party. (Excuse me—I mean PAR-TY, a noun that suddenly, without asking anybody's permission, became a verb.) Here's what you buy (please hold your applause until the end):

1. A house. Bricks and boards attractively arranged. Caring for it will consume any spare time that you have. You soon discover that you do not "own" a house; instead, the house owns you.

2. A car. But not just *any* car. A Tortellini 2000. VARROOM!!! It's the nicest toy you have ever owned. It's superbly engineered, and it drives like a dream. When the turbo kicks in, the car flattens your ears back against the headrest. A voice tells you when the door is open or the fuel level is low. It says, "Left door is ajar—Excellency." The volume control on the stereo goes from 1 to 10, and above 10 it has another setting that says: "Liquify Cerebral Cortex." It

also has some other essential yuppie accessories, like a car phone, a car fax, and a car Salad-Shooter. You squeal the tires and race the car up and down the streets. You are a race-car driver. Pocketa-pocketa-pocketa. You have learned what the difference is between a sports car and a pincushion: With a pincushion, the pinheads are on the *outside*.

3. A satellite dish. It should be at least a few more years before all broadcasters begin scrambling their signals. When that happens, you can convert your satellite dish into a bird bath for condors.

4. A Winnebago with a ballroom.

5. A video camera. Now you can pretend to be Cecil B. DeMille, George Lucas, and Steven Spielberg all rolled into one. At your last family reunion, the people with video cameras outnumbered the people without them. Everyone just stood around and filmed each other filming each other. There were some nice candid shots of a relative yelling at the children, the cat coughing up a fur ball, and people sitting in front of the TV watching videos of themselves sitting in front of the TV watching videos of themselves. You can hardly remember how boring family gatherings used to be before there were video cameras to capture all the magic on film.

Well, that's enough purchases for this week. No use becoming conspicuous about it.

These things are pretty exciting at first. After a short time, however, the thrill of these purchases wears off, and you begin looking forward to acquiring some other material thing—something that's going to make you *really* happy. Good luck. There are remedies for a bad case of the greedies, but they do not consist of feeding your habit.

Since you have to bill a lot of hours, try not to get sick. If you do get sick, be sure NOT to reveal to the doctor that you are a lawyer. Doctors and lawyers are natural enemies. If your doctor discovers that you are a lawyer, he will lunge at you with the nearest sharp instrument—a syringe, a scalpel, anything. He will scream something like, "I pay $4,000 a month in malpractice premiums, all because of LAWYERS! Doctors *never* make mistakes, but lawyers are *always* suing them! AAAAGGHHHH!!!" He will have to be subdued by his assistants and injected with a tranquilizer. So stay away from doctors. I don't know why doctors are so upset, anyway. They just pass the insurance costs on to their patients—people like you. *You* should be the one who is angry. Meanwhile, if you need an appendectomy, do it yourself. It's safer.

The Big Firm Scene

In the old days, most lawyers worked by themselves or in small firms. Now, however, some law firms have more than 1,000 lawyers. Imagine a business organization composed of 1,000 lawyers. Now think of something more pleasant—like an attack of body lice.

Some of these firms are so large they have branches all over the world. When you bring in a potential new client, you have to do a massive computer search to see whether anyone in any branch office is currently suing this client. Otherwise, your firm could end up on both sides of the litigation. This would not violate professional ethics, you understand—but some finicky clients will whine about it to the point of annoyance.

When you arrive at the firm on the first day of work, you enter a lobby that had the same designer as the Taj Mahal. The law firm sells tickets to the public just to look at it. Also, since all the senior partners demand a corner office, the building is shaped like a dodecahedron. Then they take you in the back and show you *your* office—a cubicle with a telephone. If you had wanted to work in an office like this, you would have gone into telemarketing.

If you thought that law school was rigid and hierarchical, you are in for a shock. By comparison, law school was a hippie commune. Everything in the firm operates strictly according to seniority. At the top of the food chain (or letterhead) is a senior partner, an ancient but wealthy man who is lucid only for brief moments at a time. This is the lawyer's lifelong ambition: you work until you become the senior partner. Then you die.

The firm's day-to-day operations are really governed by a Managing Committee. You have never met them, however. The only evidence that this Gang of Four exists consists of memos that periodically show up on your desk and make announcements, such as: "Beginning tomorrow all personnel shall wear uniforms to work. Please pick yours up at the supply office on the ninth floor. That is all."

Let me explain how large law firms work. The partners hire associates, pay them about a third of the income the associates bring in, and keep the rest. Naturally, the more associates and the fewer partners, the better. After the associates have billed a gazillion hours a year writing memos for seven years, the partners throw them out on their ear and hire new associates.[50] Large law firms therefore combine the best features of an indentured servitude, a sweatshop in the garment district, and a pyramid scheme.

Associates bill huge numbers of hours. Sometimes this is accomplished through "triple billing," a technique by which an associate works on client A's matter while flying to a city for client B, and he thinks that the issue may possibly somehow someday be relevant to client C. So he bills each client full bore. It is also accomplished through a time warp on the fourteenth floor, which allows associates to bill fifteen hours in a ten-hour day.

You work long hours, but it's worth it. There's nothing that compares with the quiet joy and satisfaction of helping an underprivileged megamonopoly without a friend in the world. You went into law because you wanted to help people. Now you

---

[50] During the recent economic downturn, however, law firms found that normal attrition was inadequate, and partners could be seen throwing even junior associates out of windows like sandbags.

spend most of your time swapping threats of "My robber baron can beat your robber baron." What an epic battle that would be: *The Clash of the Cretins*. Well, it's 3:00 A.M. Time to call it a day.

You work for years to become a partner in your firm. Partnership is the carrot that law firms hold out to you. Then, as you get closer to it, they either move the carrot away or slice it into smaller pieces. That's if you're lucky. If you're like most associates, they hand you a small bag of dirt and tell you to go somewhere else and grow your own carrots.

As a defense mechanism, you tell yourself that you do not intend to stay around and become a partner. You are planning to stay here just for a while, because it will look good on your résumé. You wonder whether, when you die, your résumé will be seventeen pages long, but you will never have gotten around to living. At your funeral they will bury you in the ritzy section of the cemetery, because it will look better on your résumé.

If you make partner, life is not much better than it was as an associate. The definition of a partner is a "self-employed slave." Partners spend most of their lives squabbling like a pack of hyenas over the firm's profits. This is what it means to practice at the highest level of a noble profession dedicated to the ideal of public service, to be the defenders of liberty and the architects of social worlds. It is also what it means to be a hyena.

Partnership profits are divided up according to complicated quadratic equations devised by theoretical mathematicians. The firm keeps these secret formulas locked away in the safe, so that the associates can't see how much money the partners are making off of them.

In the old days lawyers didn't worry so much about making money. They considered themselves a profession, not a business. However, things have changed, and lawyering has become more of a big business. Firms now require lawyers to work even longer hours than before, and to spend whatever free time they have digging up new business. As a result, the job satisfaction of lawyers has declined markedly in recent years. To have an easier career, many lawyers are leaving practice and getting jobs working in salt mines.

Meanwhile, legal fees have continued to climb. One reason is the rising cost of modern equipment. Law firms have bought jumbo computers that can spit out heptillions of enormous documents packed with legalese. Just a couple of keyboard strokes can bury your opponent in paper. And people once thought that technology would actually *speed up* the justice system! Ha!

Big law firms have a reputation for not giving junior people enough responsibility. The story is that the clients and the cases are so big that firms can't risk having anyone with less than fifty years' experience actually go to trial, since less senior people might blow it. This, however, is a bad rap. Many junior partners do have significant supervisory responsibilities—for example, cite-checking cases researched by the senior associates. So, law review *is* good training for big firm practice, after all.

CHAPTER
18

Areas of Practice

Lawyers specialize in many different areas. Here are a few:

LITIGATION

Litigation is the most exciting, breathtaking, heart-pounding work that lawyers do. Litigation involves something new and refreshing every day, such as:

Legal research. Junior gruntlings spend long hours in the dark recesses of the library researching obscure issues of law. They have been told that the issues somehow relate to a real client in a real lawsuit, but they have never even met the lawyer in charge of the case. For all they know, the whole assignment is a practical joke devised by some senior associate.

Document productions. These consist of two things:

1. Examining millions of documents produced by your opponents to try to figure out what documents they have withheld.
2. Producing millions of documents to your opponents in a way that conceals the documents you have withheld.

"Privileged" documents may be withheld. According to current practice, a document is "privileged" if it reveals an attorney-client communication, a trade secret, or (most importantly) any information that could possibly be damaging to your client. Many law firms have found paper shredders inadequate to handle their privileged documents. So they have replaced them with industrial incinerators.

Interrogatories. Interrogatories are thousands of subquestions smirkingly inflicted on opposing counsel. The Federal Rules of Civil Procedure prohibit interrogatories that have the purpose of causing "unnecessary delay" or "needless increase" in the cost of litigation. However, lawyers reason that *no* delay is unnecessary and *no* cost needless if it prevents their client from being held liable in court. Litigation is a war, they say, and therefore Rambo discovery tactics are proper.

Taking depositions. This involves sitting in a stuffy room crowded with stuffy lawyers, while one lawyer examines a witness who is sweating 50-caliber bullets. Since you are bored out of your skull, you casually add up the hourly billing rates of the lawyers in the room. You calculate that by the end of that day alone the legal fees in the case will exceed the annual gross income of Biloxi, Mississippi. Regrettably, the deposition will take much longer than a day. By the time all the lawyers in the room have finished examining this teenage witness, he will be drawing Social Security.

Arguing motions. Lawyers argue lots of motions, like a Motion to Strike the Opposing Party's Opposition to Your Opposition to the Opposing Party's Motion to Strike Your Motion to Compel Discovery Because a Word on the Second Page Was Misspelled. You will sit for hours (all billed to your client) in the courtroom, waiting for your turn to argue for fifteen minutes. Yep. It just doesn't get much better than this. Litigators live for glorious moments such as these.

Litigators take great pride in their ability to argue in court, and you will do the same. You speak in court without using notes: you call it "working without a net." You are so good in the courtroom that you are like a lion in a den of Daniels. You give better service per square client than any other lawyer in the state. At least, that's how you describe things to your buddies at lunch.

Negotiating settlements. Spend your time haggling over money like a street vendor in the open market. People say that's how copper wire was invented: two lawyers fighting over a penny. They also say that the difference between a lawyer and a terrorist is that you can negotiate with a terrorist. Opposing counsel threatens to sue your client if you don't settle. "Go ahead," you reply. "Lay on, Macbluff."

Going to trial. Question: What do you call a lawyer with an IQ of 50? Answer: Your Honor. Fortunately, most lawyers spend very little time with judges. The average litigator goes to trial only a couple of times in her life. In fact, some insurance defense lawyers actually pride themselves on turning a simple fender-bender into a modern version of the Thirty Years' War. Sometimes it takes so long to get to trial that by the trial date nobody can remember what the case was about. This is not a new phenomenon. The longest lawsuit on record was a case in India that took 750 years. They're actually getting pretty close to wrapping it up.

Although most lawyers rarely go to trial, I know of one lawyer who actually tried 104 cases. He lost 104 of them. When asked to explain, he answered, "You can't win 'em all."

Remember the stress of taking final exams in law school? That's what going to trial is like, except that by comparison law school exams were about as stressful as a Fourth of July picnic. This time something much more important is on the line: somebody's job (not to mention your own), millions of dollars, or even your client's life. Ulcer City. Day after day you stand in court while a grouchy judge whacks you on the head with his gavel. As a key witness testifies, the jury looks about as interested as a fourth-grade class hearing an explanation of long division. Meanwhile, the witness's own lawyer is signalling the answers to him with semaphore flags.

The story is told of a plaintiff who was seriously injured in a horse-pedestrian accident. The horse rolled over the plaintiff and broke the man's ribs, leg, and arm. On cross-examination, defense counsel asked, "Isn't it true that immediately after the accident, you told the police officer that you had never felt better?"

"Yes," the plaintiff admitted.

"Then how can you claim damages for pain and suffering?" the lawyer asked.

The plaintiff answered, "You have to understand the situation. When the police officer arrived, he drew his revolver and shot the horse. Then, with his pistol still drawn, he walked over to me and asked, 'And how are *you* feeling?' I replied that I had never felt better."

After the closing arguments, the judge reads the instructions to the jury. The instructions are statements of the applicable rules of law, and it takes the judge about two hours to read them to the jury. It took you three years of hard work in law school to learn them, but a jury right off the street is supposed to memorize them and apply them to an incredibly complex fact situation after hearing the judge read them once in a sleepy monotone. The jury then deliberates for days, and finally returns a verdict against the party whose eyes are too close together.

If litigation is a war, then litigators are the cannon fodder. High-priced cannon fodder, to be sure, but cannon fodder nonetheless. Still, under the proper circumstances, you might consider becoming a litigator. For example, if you were missing some chromosomes.

BUSINESS PRACTICE

If you thought that litigation was sedentary, you obviously aren't familiar with business practice. Some business practitioners haven't gotten up out of their chairs for two or three decades. The only indication that they're still alive is that they occasionally ask for more coffee.

Transactional work is in some respects more like business than like law. Sometimes this gets carried to extremes. Once a student interviewing at a Beverly Hills law firm asked if she could see the law library. The interviewer sniffed, "We don't do legal research here. We do deals."

Helping clients do megadeals may sound pretty exciting, but it mostly consists of cutting and pasting dreadfully boring documents. Then you get to stand by and watch as your client, who would probably be in bankruptcy without you, becomes a millionaire. Then he doesn't pay his bill.

As a business lawyer you might also do securities work, which consists largely of trying to persuade your client to disclose how much money the company is losing, how many people are suing it, what laws it has broken, and what muffinheads its directors and officers are. Since companies don't like disclosing these things (and then paying you for it), they are constantly looking for lawyers with lower standards. This is called the Trickle Down Theory. Water always seeks its own level.

REAL ESTATE WORK

Real estate lawyers become experts in the law governing dirt. It was all so easy in law school: the professor merely wrote on the blackboard, "To *A* and his heirs," and Blackacre was transferred like magic. In real (no pun intended) life (no similarity to law practice intended), you draft an insufferably long agreement that the parties bicker about for months afterward. (So why do they call it an "agreement"?) You also clear countless annoying defects off the title, as if you were picking fleas off a baboon. Then, after all this work, one party or the other backs out of the deal. Sometimes it would be easier to work with baboons.

PERSONAL INJURY

Personal injury lawyers become experts in penny-ante[51] cases in which somebody gets whiplash in the checkout line at the supermarket. In some personal injury actions, however, juries use the giant-cash-register-in-the-sky measure of damages:

> (Annual earnings of a top movie star) $\times$ (average lifespan of an Olympic athlete) + (pain, suffering, and indignity of having to deal with lawyers and wear a scratchy suit to court) $\times$ (average annual precipitation in the Brazilian rainforest) + (one-half the state budget of New Hampshire) $\times$ 150% [to give the plaintiff 100% after the lawyers take a third] $\times$ 10^{957}.

CRIMINAL DEFENSE

These are the lawyers the public hates most. According to the average person, guilty people do not deserve a trial. No, I'm just kidding—the average person does believe that criminals are entitled to a trial. And after the trial, they should be stuck with hot pokers and deported to labor camps in Greenland. After all, there is a BIG difference between criminals and law-abiding citizens. Your average citizen explains, "I pay my taxes (aside from a little chiseling on my tax return), obey the law (except for speeding, gambling, and shady business deals), and support my country (except for dodging the draft). People who actually get ARRESTED, on the other hand, are criminals. Criminals are

---

[51] The gambling metaphor is appropriate.

hairless rodents wearing clothes. Anybody will tell you that."
And everybody does.

ENVIRONMENTAL LAW

Because you love nature, you decide to go into environmental
law. You want to protect the birds, the bunnies, and the trees
from total destruction by the polluting corporate greedy-bags and
the dastardly real estate developers. But after you graduate, you
discover that most birds, bunnies, and trees don't even bother to
have a checking account. So to pursue your career in environmental law, you end up doing legal work for the polluting corporate greedy-bags and the dastardly real estate developers.
"Well, *somebody* has to do it," you tell yourself. "And it's better
if that somebody is a somebody with a conscience." So you feel
okay about yourself, as you drive your fossil-fuel-burning car
back to your redwood house in a subdivision built on a former
wetland.

TAX

Do you enjoy solving those puzzles called "Where's Waldo?",
which give you a headache and make you go nearly blind scru-
tinizing the minutest details of an incredibly complex picture?
Would you like to do that eighteen hours a day? If so, you should
become a tax lawyer. Tax lawyers spend their lives poring over
Internal Revenue regulations with a magnifying glass, looking for
hidden loopholes for their incredibly wealthy clients. Tax lawyers don't feel guilty about it. Not at all. It's a person's patriotic
duty to use the law to his or her own advantage. While it's too
bad that nonwealthy people can't afford high-priced lawyers to
help them find the loopholes, that's simply a regrettable and
extra-nifty consequence of having a free market for legal services. Besides, special interests paid good money to Congress to
get those loopholes, and it would be wasteful not to use them.
Even profligate.

ENTERTAINMENT LAW

Entertainment practice largely involves representing temperamental people in the film and music industries. These people "do lunch," "take meetings," and "have my people call your people." They also "miss" a lot of meetings. After all, "You can't push an artiste when the vibes are wrong, baby." When the deal slips away, you feel like giving them some wrongful vibes of your own.

GOVERNMENT PRACTICE

You want to pursue public good instead of private interest, so you go to work for the government. You see yourself as a modern-day Marshal Dillon, wearing a big hat and a badge. But things are different today than they were in Marshal Dillon's time. For one thing, he never had to deal with an enormous bureaucracy. You can just imagine him puzzling over the fine print in a government procedures manual: "Lemme see, here. First I have to fill out seven copies of Form 2378-50649/s-35. Then I have to transmit them to the Regional Office for preliminary approval. This will take four to six weeks. Then I . . . oh, forget it. Hey, Festus, we're gonna skip the trial. Get a rope."

Also, Marshal Dillon didn't have to deal with civil service employees. Civil service laws protect government employees from being fired for such outrageous reasons as political affiliation, the exercise of legal rights, or incompetence. These laws are just swell for *you*. Unfortunately, they also protect all the dimwits you have to work with. It's amazing you're able to get anything done at all.

PUBLIC INTEREST WORK

Here's the real reason you went to law school: you wanted to make the world a better place. So after graduation you get a job doing public interest work. Your law practice consists of comforting the afflicted and afflicting the comfortable. You also share a windowless office with seven other lawyers. Your office equipment consists of a 1963 photocopier, a manual typewriter, and a rotary-dial phone. The carpet is the color of either red or green algae, depending on how the bare light bulb over your desk shines on it.

You wanted to make the world a better place for your posterity, but right now your posterity needs such extravagant luxuries as braces, shoes, and a roof over their heads. You realize that your law degree could earn you a six-figure salary. You try to be true to your ideals, but it's hard. If only lawyers would do more pro bono work, if only government would adequately fund legal services for the poor, if only the legal system were simplified and streamlined. If only if only if only. Meanwhile, you keep working.

In law school your classmates talked a lot about doing public interest work, but most of them gradually succumbed to the siren call of big salaries and prestigious jobs. At your law school class reunion they would be *happy* to jump-start your car, but they're afraid that the jumper cables might scratch their Mercedes. "Keep up the great work," they say. "I wish I were doing it, too. See you at the next reunion."

INTERNATIONAL LAW

International work sounds inviting and enchanting. You imagine that you'll fly to fascinating foreign countries and resolve major issues in international relations, or at least facilitate exciting transnational business deals. Unfortunately, the reality of international work is something else. You find yourself discussing trademark violations on the telephone at 3:00 A.M. with some person in a country you have never heard of. He explains that you are holding the tiny candies upside down: their name is really "W & W Chocolate Candies." Your brain melts in your mouth.

ESTATE PLANNING

Estate planning lawyers spend a lot of time with people who are thinking about dying. This is an especially cheerful group of people to work with. Also, these lawyers have to keep a straight face while their client solemnly attests that he is of sound mind—while he bequeaths his entire $20 million estate to his cat, Puffles. During the ceremony, Puffles sits serenely in the chair at the other end of your office. Next to his accountant.

CHAPTER

19

Recreation for Young Professionals

Since you have been working very hard at the office, you feel a need to take a day off. But since law practice takes 180 percent of your time, it may be difficult to leave your desk even for a day. Hint: Use a hacksaw on the leg iron that shackles you to your desk. Then sneak out the back door.

The sport of preference for young professionals is currently mountain biking. However, it is an expensive and even hazardous activity, and therefore you definitely need some advice before doing it.

First, you will need to buy a mountain bike. This may be a challenge, since they are priced at about the same level as Japanese luxury sedans. They are so expensive partly because they are made of extremely lightweight metals. These metals were not even on the periodic table when you studied chemistry—metals with names like Fluffairium. Some of these metals are so light that they permit a mountain bike to actually be lighter than air.

Mountain bikes have as many as twenty-one speeds. (However, some people claim that eighteen of the speeds are simply

104

duplicates, so they're really only three-speed bikes.) Fancier mountain bikes also have "speed-shifters." These buttons permit you to shift in a single nanosecond from the very highest to the very lowest gear. You are gliding along in the highest gear, with your pedals making approximately one revolution in a twenty-four-hour period. You accidently hit the speed-shifter, and in an instant your feet have the same r.p.m. as an electric fan. This is supposed to be good for your heart.

Of course, all of this modern technology does not come cheaply. Young professionals with money to burn will spend several thousand dollars on a mountain bike. If you show up on the trail with a cheap imitation costing, say, a paltry $500, brace yourself for the consequences. These young professional adults will make you feel just like you did in the seventh grade, when everyone was wearing name-brand clothing except you. "Look," they will say, in their very responsible adult voices. "Higgins has cooties."

The bikes aren't the only equipment that these "gearheads" buy. They also buy expensive accessories, like water bottles in Day-Glo colors that do not appear anywhere on the spectrum of natural light. The bottles look like they were fished out of a toxic waste dump.

To look like an authentic mountain biker, you will need to buy some skintight clothing made of a material called spandex. Unfortunately, this clothing looks much better on other people than on you. It makes other people look very athletic. It makes you look like a hippopotamus wrapped in Saran Wrap.

You will also need to buy a helmet. Bicycle helmets are made of Styrofoam, a material with about the same protective qualities as a bag of marshmallows. However, the label assures you that the helmet works well most of the time, except that it doesn't protect against sharp objects. Fortunately, you'll encounter only a few sharp objects as you ride—sticks, rocks, and almost all of the parts of your bicycle.

Some helmets have a protective plastic coating. This prevents the helmet from bursting into flames from the friction as you skid down the road on your head. The helmet makes you look like a complete dufus, just in case the skintight clothing didn't do the trick.

When you mount the bicycle, you notice that the seat has approximately the same size—and comfort—as a nine iron. It's so small that even mosquitoes that land on it worry about falling off the edge. Place a large pillow, or maybe the mattress from your chaise lounge, over the seat.

Now start riding. The first thing you discover is that the fact that nobody has ever ridden bicycles on mountains in the entire history of the world is not exactly a complete coincidence. It's not that cyclists simply forgot that mountains existed, and now feel like total idiots, because they could have been riding on mountains instead of on paved roads without boulders and rivers and sharp rocks and cliffs and poison oak and sixty-degree grades up and down.

You are surrounded by beautiful mountain scenery, but you can't see any of it, because your eyes are glued to the four square feet of road directly in front of your bike. The vi-vi-vi-vibrations loosen every filling in your mouth.

Seeing that you are a beginner, the other cyclists will give you helpful advice. As you begin your descent down a vertical cliff, they helpfully advise you NOT to brake. "It will cause you to skid," they explain. Right now, however, skidding looks a LOT more attractive than what is about to happen, which is a free fall at thirty-two feet per second, accompanied by a loud noise bearing an uncanny resemblance to screaming. Followed by a crash.

The other riders will say, "Okay. That was a pretty good descent. Now we want you to try it while wearing the toe clips, so that you don't get tempted to put your feet down." However, you WANT to be able to put your feet down. It's not that you're chicken. It's just that your idea of a really fun time is not spending the next three weeks nursing an abrasion the size of Nebraska. So you get off the bike and go home.

You have discovered why most mountain bikes end up being resold in the secondary market—*i.e.*, garage sales presided over by smirking spouses. Bicycling was simply not designed for the mountains.

Still, a few diehards insist on riding bikes in the mountains anyway. These people can be easily identified by their thighs as thick as tree stumps and their comparatively puny little arms. They look remarkably similar to a *Tyrannosaurus rex* wearing a goofy helmet and skintight clothes. Except, of course, they no longer have any teeth.

So take my advice. Get your exercise by speed-shifting the channels with your TV remote-control. And use the money from selling your bike to buy a new mattress for your chaise lounge.

CHAPTER

20

The Unnatural Nature of the Legal Profession

Being a lawyer is like being a tour guide in a foreign country. Your clients don't know the territory or speak the language. You are their translator: you speak on their behalf and help them understand what is going on. There is one difference, however. When tourists don't like a country, they don't blame their tour guide. "I didn't invent this country," the tour guide explains. "I'm only a tour guide." If people don't like the legal system, however, they instantly blame a lawyer.

Actually, they usually don't blame their own lawyer. With some exceptions, most people believe that their own lawyer was honest and treated them fairly. It's the *other* person's lawyer who was a lying, cheating, thieving sonofagun. That should tell you something.

Part of the antagonism toward lawyers is, quite frankly, based on partisanship. People see in the media a lawyer advocating a position with which they disagree, or representing a client who is guilty. They know the client is guilty because they have read all about it in the newspapers. These newspapers are written by reporters the public also doesn't trust, which creates a puzzling logical conundrum. In any event, to mix a metaphor, that's when the can of worms hits the fan. That's when people become mere pawns in a much larger ballgame. For some reason, the opposition forces are personified in the lawyer who is the advocate. People feel slightly better when they see another lawyer advocating a position with which they agree. "Now there's a lawyer you can trust," they say. "If only more lawyers were like her."

Still, negative reactions often tend to be stronger than positive ones, and many people are left with negative impressions about lawyers in general. They use a silent syllogism: since my position is eminently reasonable, the lawyer on the other side must be either dumb or dishonest, either a fool or a knave. The public generally perceives lawyers as being smart. Therefore, the only conclusion is that they must be corrupt.

The truth is that lawyers are about as honest as other people, given their opportunities. Unfortunately, they have many more opportunities than most people to be dishonest. But when people read about a (supposedly) frivolous case asking for millions of dollars in damages, they think, "Those darn lawyers." They should think, "Those darn Americans. We sure are becoming a greedy society."

But the lawyers know better, the reasoning goes. Because of their training and knowledge, we expect more of them. We do, and we should. But to blame one segment of society for all of society's ills is an old trick. If our society is too greedy, too dishonest, too litigious, too uncivil, then blaming one group or another is a copout. We as a society should look in the mirror. In good lighting. And not angle our head just right, like we always do, so that our defects don't show.

Meanwhile, one economist asserts that each lawyer costs the nation one million dollars per year in lost gross national product.[52] So I say, Give me a cool $800,000, and I'll go home. We pay farmers not to grow crops, don't we?

---

[52] *See An Economist Out to Be Sued*, L.A. Times, Oct. 8, 1990, at D1.

CHAPTER
21

Lawyers Throughout History

Most people do not appreciate the crucial role that lawyers have played throughout history. Lawyers have been present at nearly every important event since the very beginning. Here are only a few examples:

ADAM AND EVE

EVE: What's this in the mailbox? It's a "Three-day Notice to Quit the Premises." It says we have just three days to leave the Garden of Eden or we'll be forcibly evicted.

ADAM: How can that be?

EVE: It claims that we have breached one of the covenants in the lease—something about eating a forbidden fruit.

ADAM: Oh, that. That can't be a material breach, can it?

THE DEVIL, ESQ.: Let me handle this. I can tie this thing up in the courts forever.

ADAM: What's that thundering noise?

NOAH'S ARK

LAWYER: What are you doing?

NOAH: I'm leading these animals into the ark.

LAWYER: I represent an animal rights organization. You can't put those animals in those cramped quarters. You'll have to cut some windows in that boat.

NOAH: I don't know. Windows in an ark don't sound like a very good idea to me.

LAWYER: Get those animals out of there, or I'll get a temporary restraining order. And hurry up. It's starting to rain.

MOSES

MOSES: I command that the water . . .

LAWYER: Hey! Stop that!

MOSES: But I was about to divide the Red Sea, so we can escape from Pharaoh's army.

LAWYER: Not without first filing an Environmental Impact Statement, you don't. Can you imagine what might happen to the aquatic life in the Red Sea if you divide it?

MOSES: Can you imagine what will happen to the human life all around me if I don't?

LAWYER: Wait a minute. You're the same guy who turned the Nile River into blood and caused the frogs, lice, flies, hail, fire, locusts, and darkness. The environmental officials are going to levy some pretty stiff fines on you, pal.

MOSES: Well, we have to be going. You wait here for the chariots. Perhaps you can even catch a ride with them.

CONFUCIUS

CONFUCIUS: He who chops his own wood is warmed twice.

LAWYER: You can't say it that way. It's not completely accurate, and you open yourself to liability.

CONFUCIUS: How should I say it?

LAWYER: A person who chops wood may experience a temporary rise in body temperature. Be sure to use proper equipment and protective clothing when chopping wood, including a sharp ax, boots, gloves, and protective eyewear. Do not chop any parts of your body, as this can cause severe

injuries. Do not chop wood if you are under the influence of alcohol or medication. You should have a physical examination before engaging in strenuous exercise. Burning wood can produce a temporary increase in room temperature. Burn the wood only in an approved fireplace. Do not stand too close to the fire. Do not let children burn wood without adult supervision. Extinguish the fire completely before leaving it unsupervised. This wise saying is presented "as is"—Confucius makes no warranties, expressed or implied, and in no event will be liable for any direct or consequential damages. Some states do not allow a limitation on warranties, so your remedies may vary.

CONFUCIUS: I don't know. I kind of like the simpler version better.

LAWYER: Trust me. Otherwise, how are you ever going to make a name for yourself?

COLUMBUS

COLUMBUS: The world is round, and I intend to sail to India. But I need financing from Your Majesty.

QUEEN ISABELLA: I'm willing to help.

LAWYER: Wait. If you're going to raise financing, you have to file a prospectus with the SEC. It must describe the background and expertise of every sailor in your crew, detail the nature of all your physical equipment and other assets, provide audited income statements and balance sheets for each of the last three fiscal years, and disclose all the risks of the voyage.

COLUMBUS: I don't have the money to do all that. That's why I'm here.

LAWYER: Your Majesty, this is obviously an undercapitalized business venture. I cannot recommend an investment of any kind in it.

QUEEN ISABELLA: Lock the lawyer in the hold of the *Santa Maria*, and don't let him out until you reach land. Then leave him there.

SHAKESPEARE

LAWYER: Are you William Shakespeare?

SHAKESPEARE: To be or not to be. Is that the question?

LAWYER: Here is a court order closing the Globe Theatre.

SHAKESPEARE: This is the unkindest cut of all. Why is this happening?

LAWYER: The plots in some of your plays aren't original. The copyright owners are shutting you down. Also, you are guilty of urging people to kill all the lawyers. That's inciting a riot.

SHAKESPEARE: Alas, our fate lies not in ourselves but in our lawyers.

LAWYER: Cut out the theatrics. You've presented your last play, Bill. Someday the world will thank me.

THE AMERICAN REVOLUTION

PATRICK HENRY: As for me, give me liberty, or give me death!

LAWYER: Well, we may not like the king's decrees, but they *are* the law.

PATRICK HENRY: Of course *you* defend them; you love having lots of unjust laws to enforce and litigate over.

LAWYER: It's a living. Besides, I get to wear these nifty powdered wigs.

THE LOUISIANA PURCHASE

PRESIDENT JEFFERSON: I'll just sign my name here, and the Louisiana Purchase will be complete.

LAWYER: I advise against it. First we should do a title search.

PRESIDENT JEFFERSON: How long will that take?

LAWYER: It's a pretty big piece of property—I'd say about 250 years.

PRESIDENT JEFFERSON: Like I said, I'll just sign my name here . . .

LAWYER: It's irresponsible. You're not even buying title insurance.

PRESIDENT JEFFERSON: You know, I've always wondered whether a quill pen is strong enough to pierce a human skull . . .

KITTY HAWK

ORVILLE: Wilbur, we're almost ready to take off. Hold the wing steady.

LAWYER: Excuse me, Mr. Wright. Have you thought about the documents you should prepare before you begin the age of flight?

ORVILLE: What documents?

LAWYER: Patents, articles of incorporation, licenses with appropriate federal and state agencies, flight plans, safety inspection reports, insurance forms, applications for air routes, labor contracts, noncompetition agreements, income tax forms. These are just a few.

ORVILLE: I just want to see if the thing will fly. And if you don't stop yammering at me, I'll never get it off the ground.

LAWYER: I can't help it. I get paid by the yammer.

WATERGATE

Wait a minute. Most of the defendants in Watergate *were* lawyers. It's too tragic to be funny.

AND FINALLY, THE FUTURE:
THE FINAL JUDGMENT

LAWYER: I tried to strike a plea bargain to get you into heaven, but it didn't work. Your rap sheet is too long. It leaves *nothing* out.

CLIENT: Didn't I do *anything* good in my life?

LAWYER: Well, you did give $3.75 to an orphanage once. And I pointed that out.

CLIENT: So what's the best you could do for me?

LAWYER: They said they would be willing to refund your $3.75 and tell you to go to hell. But it's not so bad. I only got $2.42.

CHAPTER

Where Our Laws Come From

Where do our laws come from? The answer is: from government. (Pronounced "govment." Executive Order No. 3257 signed by Jimmy Carter and extended by Ronald Reagan.)

Under the Constitution, there are three branches of the federal government: the Moe Branch, the Curly Branch, and the Larry Branch. No, it's unfair to compare the federal government to the Three Stooges. Curly would be offended.

The federal government is more like the story of the Three Little Pigs. There is the House of Straw (Congress), the House of Sticks (the Executive Branch), and the House of Bricks (the Judiciary). Not all fairy tales begin with "Once upon a time." Some of them begin with "If I get elected . . . ."

The voters are like the Big Bad Wolf. They get REALLY REALLY mad, and they HUFF, and they PUFF, and they threaten to blow everyone's house down. But they never do, basically because the Three Little Pigs keep dishing up pork barrel as fast as they can and feeding it to the Big Bad Wolf. Here is a description of our government:

THE EXECUTIVE BRANCH

The Constitution specifies that the President's duties are to:

1. Propose legislation for Congress to reject, and veto any legislation that Congress passes.
2. a. Attend funerals of foreign dignitaries.
   b. Attend funerals of domestic dignitaries.
   c. Try to avoid attending his *own* funeral.
3. Invade underdeveloped countries if they get uppity.
4. When the pressures of the job get to the President, do what any average American would do: fly to his ranch or beach house for a four-week vacation.

The Executive Branch also contains countless minions who work in the federal agencies, and who decide weighty matters of state, such as which flavor of glue should be placed on the back of postage stamps. They also consider important regulatory measures, like forcing people to put a pollution-control device on their gasoline lawn mower. This was a real proposal. I previously opposed mandatory drug testing for federal employees, but not anymore.

THE LEGISLATIVE BRANCH

Congress contains two groups of people: liberals and conservatives. Liberals want to regulate business activity but not sexual conduct, while conservatives want precisely the opposite. In short, each group wants to regulate the other.

Congress is the object of a lot of unfair criticism. Members of Congress are merely the employees of the American people. Unfortunately, it is REALLY difficult to work for 250 million bosses. Working for only one boss is enough to drive most people to homicide. Working for millions of them makes members of Congress want to wrestle the nuclear "football" away from the President and blow up their entire voting district.

Soon after they are elected, members of Congress discover that they only need two things to get reelected: money and votes. Therefore, Congress tends to pay a LOT more attention to those particular bosses who can deliver either money or votes. Preferably within thirty minutes.

In doing this, Congress divides Americans into two groups: (1) People with a lot of money; and (2) People with little or no money. The first group has a lot of money but few votes. So Congress accepts money from that group and then pays special attention to what that group wants. Of course, Congress insists that it is not influenced AT ALL by what that group wants. According to this view, Congress is one of the few places where people accept large sums of money from total strangers and are not expected to do anything in return. The second group has many votes but little money. So Congress buys their votes with federal programs, public benefits, and pork barrel. Of course— and here's the trick—buying these votes doesn't cost Congress one cent. Congress buys the votes with the voters' *own* money. Pretty slick, huh? Yep. About as slick as a perpetual motion machine. It looks like it's working just fine, but unfortunately it violates the laws of math and physics.

The voters want two things:

1. Lots of public programs and benefits; and
2. Low taxes.

So Congress gives them exactly those things. Of course, this creates a federal deficit of more than $300 billion a year. Congress just puts the tab on a credit card the size of New Jersey. Someone else will pay for it, they say. Someone still too young to vote.

Then, however, the voters get hopping mad because the budget deficit is getting as massive as some of the larger planets in our solar system. "DO SOMETHING ABOUT IT," they scream, "or we'll vote you out of office. But don't raise our taxes or cut our benefits, or we'll vote you out of office. Raise someone else's taxes. Cut someone else's benefits. Are you people cretins, or what?" Then, when the budget deficit worsens, the voters want to throw all the bums out. Well, not ALL the bums. They want to throw out EVERYONE ELSE'S incumbent, but keep their OWN incumbent ("Pork Barrel Bob") in Congress. After all, he delivers for their district.

So there's the stalemate. The problem is not Congress; it's us. We believe that government is so powerful it can do anything— even violate the laws of mathematics. Meanwhile, the best that Congress can come up with is the Gramm-Rudman deficit-reduction law, a statute that says, "Stop me before I kill again."

So Congress spends its time in more productive pursuits—like going on fact-finding tours to beautiful Caribbean islands. By sheer coincidence, most of these facts are scattered along the beach or on golf courses. But that's not Congress's fault.

THE JUDICIARY

According to the Constitution, the duties of Supreme Court justices are to:

1. Strike down laws they don't like.
2. Announce that they really *like* the laws they're striking down—honestly and truly—but their hands are tied by some secret principle of constitutional law that nobody has ever thought of before.
3. Remind the public in solemn tones that, since they were never elected and can't ever be voted out of office, they can NEVER EVER substitute their own policy choices for those of the people's duly elected representatives. Otherwise our country would be governed by themselves—a small clot of unelected lawyers.
4. Go back into their chambers and fall on the floor in hysterical fits of laughter.

The Court is also pretty tricky with math. In its dealings with Congress over the years, the Court has proved many times that $9 > 535$. Often the mystical qualities of the Court's decisions have demonstrated the supremacy of the transcendental numbers over the irrational numbers.

STATE AND LOCAL GOVERNMENTS

Under the Constitution, state and local governments are supposed do most of the governing, under the theory that they are closer to the people and more responsive to their wishes. And since nowadays most people's wishes are to receive more services and pay lower taxes, state and local governments currently spend most of their time doing what patriotic citizens everywhere do—asking Congress for more money. Congress will, in turn, finance these requests through increased deficit spending. Americans believe that we really can, if we try hard enough, borrow enough money to get ourselves completely out of debt.

CHAPTER
23

An Unofficial Guide to
the Bill of Rights

One of the cornerstones of freedom in America is the Bill of Rights. Actually, the official name is the "William of Rights," but we have affectionately come to call it "Bill" for short. It should not be confused with the "Morty of Rights" or the "Louise of Rights," which are different things altogether.[53] The news media usually refer to the fundamental liberties in the Bill of Rights as "technicalities."

The Bill of Rights consists of ten amendments:

The First Amendment has several clauses. The establishment clause prohibits religious displays by the government, unless they are accompanied by Rudolf the Red-Nosed Reindeer.[54] Apparently, Rudolph's nose talismanically wards off both good and evil spirits.

[53] Rimshot.
[54] You don't believe me? *Compare* County of Allegheny v. ACLU, 492 U.S. 573 (1989) (county's display of crèche surrounded by floral decorations was unconstitutional) *with* Lynch v. Donnelly, 465 U.S. 668 (1984) (city's display of crèche along with reindeer, Santa Claus, and other items representing winter holiday traditions was constitutional).

The free exercise clause, according to a recent Supreme Court case,[55] generously permits you to have whatever religious beliefs you want. You just can't "exercise" them. It's comforting to know that the protection of religious liberty in America is now just as broad as it is in NORTH KOREA.

Whereas the free exercise clause specifically mentions but does not protect conduct, the free speech clause does not mention conduct but protects it. However, the Court's decisions protecting flag burning[56] have been extremely unpopular. Fortunately for the Court, it has not yet held that the First Amendment protects the burning of SUPREME COURT JUSTICES in effigy.

The Second Amendment means that you do NOT have the right to bear arms—unless you are a militia, like the KKK or the Mafia. When those militias come around, the rest of us are limited to shooting at them with rubber bands and peashooters.

Conservatives, however, argue that the amendment's reference to a well-regulated militia was REALLY intended to protect the use of automatic weapons to defend against the local deer population. After all, you never know when you'll be walking down the street and run into a left-wing fawn ("Bambo") armed with a BAZOOKA. Conservatives believe that the Second Amendment is the ONLY amendment that applies to the states, under a doctrine called "bull's-eye incorporation."

The Third Amendment means that soldiers cannot be drawn and quartered in private homes. We have boot camps for that.

The Fourth Amendment means that criminals have the right to be secure in their persons, houses, and effects. Consequently, none of the rest of us are.

The Fifth Amendment has several clauses. The double jeop-

---

[55] Employment Div. v. Smith, 494 U.S. 872 (1990) (free exercise clause does not create exemptions from general criminal laws regulating conduct).

[56] United States v. Eichman, 496 U.S. 310 (1990) (flag burning as a mode of expression is protected by the First Amendment); Texas v. Johnson, 491 U.S. 397 (1980) (flag burning during protest rally was expressive conduct protected by the First Amendment).

ardy clause protects a person from being put in jeopardy of life or limb twice. To some justices, this means that nobody can be put in jeopardy of life or limb EVEN ONCE. These justices plausibly explain that even though the Constitution specifically mentions "capital" crimes, it means crimes committed in state capitals.

The self-incrimination clause protects criminals from the unspeakable cruelty, presently banished in all civilized societies, of having to tell the truth in the presence of a judge.

The due process clause entitles a person to "due substance." In the first part of this century conservatives claimed that the substance included economic liberties, pointing out that the Constitution specifically mentions economic rights. However, liberals ridiculed that method of interpretation as simply politics. To return some neutrality and legitimacy to the process, liberals replaced that method with a MUCH less political method which permits them to find rights not mentioned anywhere in the Constitution.

The just compensation clause means that you have the right to become rich if you own a patch of worthless desert in the path of an interstate freeway. However, if the state legislature puts your coal mine out of business, your only option is to turn it into a summer resort for vampires and their lawyers.[57] (Wait a minute; that phrase may be redundant.)

The Sixth Amendment guarantees several things. It guarantees defendants the right to a speedy and public trial, even though most of them protest loudly. It guarantees the right to be tried by a bright and intelligent jury of people who never read newspapers or watch television. And the right to counsel pretty much guarantees full employment for lawyers for the duration of the Republic.

The Seventh Amendment preserves the right to a jury trial when the amount in controversy exceeds twenty dollars. I think

---

[57] *See* Keystone Bituminous Coal Ass'n v. DeBenedictis, 480 U.S. 470 (1987) (Pennsylvania regulation requiring that 50% of coal beneath certain structures be kept in place does not constitute a taking).

that the dollar amount should be linked to the Consumer Price Index. In 1791, twenty dollars would buy a carriage and a team of fine horses. Today it will buy two hamsters and an exercise wheel.

The Eighth Amendment prohibits cruel and unusual punishments, which have been held to include most of the punishments the framers liked best. Regrettably, it does not include the worst punishment of all: being forced to spend an entire evening in a locked room with an Amway sales representative.

The Ninth Amendment states that enumerating certain rights in the Constitution does not deny other rights retained by the people. If you can figure out what those other rights are, you are a genius. Or a liberal.

Finally, the Tenth Amendment provides that the powers not delegated to the United States are reserved to the states or to the people. For example, if by some freak accident Congress actually balances the federal budget some day, you will still have the right to go into bankruptcy yourself. This amendment means that members of Congress are not the only people entitled to make fools of themselves.

The Bill of Rights was originally intended to apply only to the federal government, but the Court has applied some amendments to the states, under the doctrine of incorporation. This doctrine has been defined as a magic sleight-of-hand in which a nine-justice prestidigitator chooses a number between one and ten and changes it into a fourteen.[58]

But then again, it's not the only time that the Court has dabbled in magic. And with all this judicial magic, what I want to know is this: where is Rudolph's nose when we really need it?

---

[58] Robert J. Morris, Comment, *The New (Legal) Devil's Dictionary*, 6 J. Contemp. L. 231, 233 (1979).

Conclusion

So now you know all there is to know about law school and the legal profession. If you haven't yet decided whether to go to law school, you should consider it carefully. If you are in law school or are a lawyer already, you should also consider your options. But if you want my objective, even-handed, carefully considered advice, I'll tell you:

GET THE HEY OUT OF IT WHILE YOU STILL CAN!!!

Epilogue

For a moment I would like to say a few serious things about lawyers and lawyering. All kidding aside, the law is a noble profession, one that is indispensable to the functioning of our society. Still, the nature of the profession is such that distant observers will often not understand how or why it works.

This fact can be illustrated in a story by Robert Louis Stevenson. In the evenings when he was a boy, Stevenson and his friends copied British police officers by carrying small, tin bull's-eye lanterns on their belts. Just for the fun of it, the boys made a game out of hiding a glowing lantern inside the front of their buttoned overcoats and then making their way in the dark as if they had no light with them. In Stevenson's words,

> When two of these [youths] met, there would be an anxious "Have you got your lantern?" and a gratified "Yes!" That was the shibboleth, and very needful; for, as it was the rule to keep our glory contained, none could recognise a lantern-bearer . . . .
>
> The essence of this bliss was to walk by yourself in the black night; the slide shut, the top-coat buttoned; not a ray escaping, whether to conduct your footsteps or to make your glory public: a mere pillar of darkness in the dark; and all the while, deep down in the privacy of your fool's heart, to know you had a bull's-eye at your belt, and to exult and sing over the knowledge.
>
> . . . [One's] life from without may seem but a rude mound

of mud; [but] there will be some golden chamber at the heart of it, in which he dwells delighted; and for as dark as his pathway seems to the observer, he will have some kind of a bull's-eye at his belt.[59]

This is a private kind of joy. But it is so significant that Stevenson says, "[T]o miss the joy is to miss all. In the joy of the actors lies the sense of any action. That is the explanation, that is the excuse. To one who has not the secret of the lanterns, the scene [of the young people in the darkness] is meaningless."[60]

The joy of making a difference—a real difference, a difference that means something in the lives of other people—is what makes the practice of law worthwhile. Being of service is the best reason for going into law.

Lawyers are an elite. The legal profession includes some of the best educated and most powerful people in our society. Lawyers should be under no delusion that they have earned these privileges entirely on their own. No one can justifiably take personal pride in inborn abilities that he or she received free of charge. Also, one's educational opportunities often have much more to do with where and when one was born than with meritocracy.

Lawyers should not measure their self-worth by the fact that they are well educated, wealthy, or powerful. In the ultimate calculus, virtue matters much more than worldly achievements. But if that is true, what of a person's efforts toward competence, and even excellence, in the study and practice of law? I believe that lawyers have a duty to develop their talents and to use them to serve others. Striving for excellence is not incompatible with that goal. Increasing one's abilities increases one's abilities to serve.

In Chaim Potok's novel *The Chosen*,[61] Reb Saunders had a

---

[59] Robert Louis Stevenson, *The Lantern-Bearers*, in 2 *The Works of Robert Louis Stevenson* 548–49 (1910).

[60] *Id.* at 554.

[61] Chaim Potok, *The Chosen* (1967).

brilliant son, Danny. Danny had "a mind like a jewel," "like a pearl, like a sun." Reb Saunders explained,

> [W]hen my Daniel was four years old, I saw him reading a story from a book. And I was frightened. He did not read the story, he swallowed it, as one swallows food or water. . . . It was a story in a Yiddish book about a poor Jew and his struggles . . . . Ah, how that man suffered! And my Daniel *enjoyed* the story, he *enjoyed* the last terrible page, because when he finished it he realized for the first time what a memory he had. He looked at me proudly and told me back the story from memory, and I cried inside my heart. . . . "A mind like this I need for a son? A *heart* I need for a son, a *soul* I need for a son, *compassion* I want from my son, righteousness, mercy, strength to suffer and carry pain, *that* I want from my son, not a mind without a soul."[62]

Reb Saunders feared that Danny would have a cold mind, a cruel mind—proud, haughty, impatient with less brilliant minds, unable to understand pain, indifferent to suffering. Therefore, he imposed upon his son a regimen of silence, so that Danny could learn of pain and understand the pain of others. In this manner, Reb Saunders hoped to teach Danny to suffer for his people, to take their pain from them, and to carry it on his own shoulders.

Good lawyers must have the skills required for professional competence. But this is not enough. They must know how to carry the burdens of other people on their shoulders. They must know of pain, and how to help heal it. Lawyers can be healers. Like physicians, ministers, and other healers, lawyers are persons to whom people open up their innermost secrets when they have suffered or are threatened with serious injury.[63] People go to them to be healed, to be made whole, and to be protected

---

[62] *Id.* at 264–65.
[63] Bruce C. Hafen, To Beginning Law Students on "Professionalism" 5 (unpublished manuscript).

from harm.[64] These are large and important tasks, and they require all that lawyers have to offer. They require both good minds and good hearts—not only mental acuity and professional skill, but also compassion, righteousness, mercy, and strength to suffer and carry pain. That is what it takes to be a truly good lawyer. And the world desperately needs truly good lawyers.

[64] *See id.*

A Glossy Glossary of Legal Terms

Abatable nuisance. A law professor without tenure.

Abuse of discretion. The law school grading system.

Acceleration. Self-help remedy to avoid repossession when you miss a payment on your Corvette.

Ad hoc. Sound made by a country lawyer spitting.

Adverse possession. Legal rule providing that the bold shall inherit the earth.

Affidavit. A written statement under oath that is so true that the affiant prefers not to appear in court and be questioned about it.

Aforementioned. The thing I've told you four times already. *Cf.* athreementioned.

Alienation of affections. What happens to a marriage when one spouse becomes a lawyer.

Allegation. An assertion made by an alligator.

Alter ego. The one other than the ego, the super ego, and the id. *Cf.* the Statute of Freuds.

Alternative pleading. The classic example is: My client was out of town on the day of the murder. And if he wasn't, he was not at the scene of the crime. And if he was, he didn't pull the trigger. And if he did, he's insane.

Ambiguity. Something with a double or uncertain meaning. Legal reasoning consists mostly of reshuffling the ambiguities.

Amicus curiae. Latin for "My friend can be cured." A brief filed by a nonparty to a lawsuit who realizes that the real parties are going to blow it.

Anticipatory breach. A repudiation of a contractual obligation before it is due. *E.g.*, when a restaurant patron dumps his bowl of spaghetti on the waiter's head, it's a pretty good indication that he does not intend to pay for it.

Antitrust laws. Statutes prohibiting companies from becoming powerful octopus-like monopolies through mergers and acquisitions. The government forgot about these laws during the 1980's.

Assumption of risk. Matriculation in law school.

Bankruptcy. Consists primarily of two kinds: (1) Chapter 7, in which the creditors divide the remaining assets immediately; and (2) Chapter 11, in which the lawyers do it over the next two decades.

Bill of particulars. A more definite statement in a lawsuit. For example, if the plaintiff alleged, "The defendant did intentionally and wantonly inflict emotional harm on the plaintiff, causing him intense and severe pain and suffering and injuring him in an amount not less than 50 million dollars," the defendant could request a bill of particulars. The plaintiff would then have to specify that the defendant called him a dodo.

Breach of contract. Something somebody else always does first, just like the fights you had with your siblings when you were a child.

Breach of warranty. There should be a photograph of a Yugo here.

Burden of proof. The eleven-foot stack of documents the clerk has to carry out of the courtroom at the end of even the simplest trial.

Caveat emptor. Latin for "Let the buyer empty the cave." Used when prehistoric buyers purchased a cave without realizing that the sellers had kept their bison in the back room for years.

Chain of title. The bondage that occurs in a slow market when you can't sell your house and escape your huge mortgage.

Chancery. (1) The jurisprudence exercised in a court of equity. (2) A state lottery, which is more predictable.

Chattel. A movable thing, such as the real estate located along the San Andreas fault.

Circuit court. A source of electrifying jurisprudence. *Cf.* short-circuit court.

Civil litigation. An oxymoron. *Cf.* civil war, marital bliss, family vacation, honest lawyer, professional wrestling, speedy trial, original copy, water landing, TV guest host, reasonable attorney's fees, interesting professor, and good law school.

Class action. A lawsuit brought by people who don't even know it. Employed because the number of people willing to sue is, incredibly, still too small to satisfy lawyers.

Cogent argument. An argument formed by dividing the short side of the triangle by the hypotenuse. *Cf.* tangential argument.

Collateral source rule. The rule providing that the law school will not give you financial aid if any of your relatives to the seventh degree of consanguinity have any money.

Common carrier. *E.g.*, trains and airlines. Because of the economy, becoming less common every day.

Compelling interest. The paramount interest the government must have to override certain constitutional rights. According to the current Supreme Court, administrative convenience is more than enough to satisfy the test.

Concur. Latin for "with a dog." *E.g.*, "I agree with the court's result, but I've seen better reasoning from a dachshund."

Confession. Something that occurs only outside of the presence of a lawyer. It is usually given voluntarily, after the police have improved the defendant's uncooperative attitude with electroshock therapy.

Consideration. Something of value that is bargained for. In general, a promise requires consideration to be binding. This requirement produces the silly consequence of making many contractual modifications unenforceable. Approved by the British House of Lords, this doctrine was the result of generations of inbreeding among the aristocracy, which had a debilitating effect on rational thought.

Contemporary community standards. The background against which to test whether something is obscene. The phrase is increasingly oxymoronic.

Contingent fee. Form of legalized gambling in a lottery administered by the judiciary. Only lawyers may play.

Contributory negligence. The common law rule that one moron may not sue another. It has been largely replaced by comparative negligence, in which the parties desperately try to prove each other the bigger moron.

Corpus delicti. A compliment paid by a cannibal to his dinner host. *E.g.*, "This corpus is delicti."

Court-martial. Compared to nonmilitary proceedings, a legal proceeding from Mars.

Covenant not to compete. Solemn agreement entered into by the backbenchers in a law school class.

Cruel and unusual punishment. The kind of punishment banned by the Eighth Amendment. Grammatically, any punishment, no matter how cruel, is constitutional if it is used often enough.

Data. Scientific evidence introduced in court. Latin for "the plural of anecdote."

De jure. Latin for "the world as law professors describe it." *Cf.* de facto, "the world as it really is."

Demurrer. Based on the Latin word *dimorari*, meaning "to delay." I am not kidding.

Dictum. A court's remark not necessary to the decision of the case. *E.g.,* "Counsel's suit looks like it fit better on the camel."

Diminished capacity. Mental defect short of insanity. Polite description of opposing counsel's intelligence.

Discovery. The formal process of obtaining information and evidence from an adverse party. For most lawyers, this is the only kind of fishing expedition they will ever have time for.

Diversity of citizenship. Because a person from one state might be treated unfairly in the courts of another state, the Constitution permits that person to sue a citizen of the other state in federal court. However, nobody realized that both the federal judge and the federal jury would still come from the other state. Picky, picky, picky.

Doe, John or Jane. After you have already sued everybody listed in the municipal telephone directory, a name you add to catch any new move-ins.

Domicile. During law school, the library.

En banc. (Pronounced "on bonk.") When the full court gets together to bonk one of its judges on the head for screwing up the law.

Entrapment. What gradually happens to students who begin law school with the goal of a career in public interest work.

Equity. The value of your house minus its mortgage, the preservation of which is the only reason you have to get up in the morning and go to work.

Escheat. Something politicians do to their espouses.

Esquire. Pretentious title used by Anglophile lawyers who wish they had lived three centuries ago in Britain. If they had, they probably would have worked as serfs to esquires.

Estop. To stop. A word invented by lawyers paid by the syllable.

Execute. (1) To sign a legal document. (2) What your senior partner does to you when you show him the document you have drafted for the firm's major client.

Ex post facto. How the common law works. Jeremy Bentham observed that the common law treats a person like he treats his dog: he waits until it does something wrong, and then he kicks it.

Felony murder rule. A rule providing that a homicide committed during a felony is automatically a first-degree murder. Under this rule, a getaway driver gets the electric chair if his buddies unexpectedly waste the convenience store clerk, even though all he wanted out of the whole thing was a box of Milk Duds.

Feudalism. *See* Large law firm.

First impression. Refers to the first time an issue is considered by a court. *Cf.* last impression, which refers to constitutional rights under the current Supreme Court.

Forms of action. Old-fashioned legal proceedings. Puttin' on the writs.

Forum non conveniens. Latin for "The Forum is not convenient." The reason why 7-Elevens sprang up all over ancient Rome.

Frivolous argument. A quark—something so light it has no mass and so simple it has no internal structure. Yet it is one of the basic building blocks of legal atomic structure.

Frivolous suit. A seersucker suit. *Cf.* Sincere sucker suit.

Full faith and credit. The hope that you will someday be able to pay off your student loans.

Good faith. Honesty in fact. *Cf.* Honesty in law.

Guest statute. Law prohibiting a nonpaying passenger from recovering damages for negligence from the car's driver. We have crime, drugs, and homelessness in our society, and instead our government elects to spend its efforts trying to eliminate the monstrous evil of ingratitude.

Habeas corpus. Latin for "You have the body." An ancient Roman pickup line.

Hearsay. True things said outside of court that are too juicy for the jury to hear.

Ignoratia legis non excusat. Latin for "Ignorance of the law is no excuse." Clever remark written by your professor on your exam answer.

Impanelling. (1) The process of selecting and swearing in jurors. (2) What you accidentally did to your youngest child when you finished the basement of your house.

Inclusio unius est exclusio alterius. Latin for "Inclusion of one is exclusion of another." *E.g.*, law practice, and a life.

Indispensable party. An annual ordeal sponsored by your firm's senior partner, the absence from which is unforgivable.

In extremis. Latin for "in anticipation of death." The feeling you get a half hour before the bar exam.

In forma pauperis. Latin for "in the manner of a pauper." Your lifestyle during law school. You have so little money that your shoes are carved out of zucchini. However, it's not so bad. A good pair of zucchini shoes will last two weeks before they get too mushy to walk in.

In loco parentis. Latin for "crazy parent." You, after spending a rainy weekend indoors with your kids.

In pari delicto. Latin for "These pears are delicious." Often employed to change the subject when your client tries to bring up legal matters at lunch.

In pari materia. Latin for "dropping the pears on your client's clothes." Employed if *in pari delicto* is unsuccessful.

In rem jurisdiction. A topic in Civil Procedure that induces rapid-eye-movement stages of sleep.

Insanity. The condition of having lost one's mind. A jury once found a defendant not guilty by reason of insanity, but they backed down when the judge asked, "What? All twelve of you?"

Insider trading. Method of income supplementation for corporate officers who follow the advice of George Washington Plunkitt: "I seen my opportunities and I took 'em."

Insurable interest. A relationship with a person or thing that will support the issuance of an insurance policy. This requirement prevents mobsters from taking out insurance on your life before they resort to self-help to collect on your debt.

Intentional infliction of emotional distress. Jokingly telling your study partner that you accidentally lost her Civil Procedure outline.

In toto. Where Dorothy's ruby slippers ended up.

Joinder. The uniting of several causes of action or parties in a single suit. Joinder rules have become very liberal. Experts predict that by the year 2010 all living Americans will actually be parties in the same humongous lawsuit.

Justice of the peace. A double oxymoron.

Last clear chance. The deadline for the GMAT, which would permit you to get an MBA instead of going to law school.

Law merchant. Public relations employee in a large law firm.

Leading question. A question which suggests the answer. *E.g.,* "The light was green, wasn't it?" After opposing counsel objects, the lawyer can then ask precisely the same question in a nonleading way. By this time, of course, any witness with the IQ of a pretzel knows the answer the lawyer is looking for.

Lex loci. Evil villain in Superman comics.

Long-arm statute. (1) A law that permits a court to obtain jurisdiction over a nonresident. (2) A law that measures arm length to make sure that professional football teams consist only of *Homo sapiens*. This law does not apply to professional wrestling.

May it please the court. Formal opening of an argument, meaning "Your esteemed imbecile."

Meeting of minds. The mutual manifestation of assent to the terms of a contract. It is not required that the parties' minds actually meet, or even that they have minds. Otherwise, no one could make an enforceable contract to buy a Chia Pet.

Nemo est supra legis. Latin for "Only Captain Nemo is above the law."

Nominal damages. The kind of damages juries used to award, when compared to the amount they routinely award today.

Oral contract. According to Samuel Goldwyn, a contract not worth the paper it's not written on.

Parade of horribles. (1) A list of possible negative consequences. (2) The annual Halloween parade in Transylvania.

Parole evidence rule. A rule that bars the admission of oral evidence when there is a written contract. The rule is based on the remarkable assumption that people never speak when they negotiate and sign contracts. However, this assumption is true of form contracts, which nobody ever explains.

Pendente lite. A beer advertising campaign directed at young lawyers.

Person. Legal category that includes not only human beings but also nonhuman entities, such as law review editors.

Possibility of a reverter. The slim chance that you'll remember anything about estates on your Property exam.

Precedent. Prior cases. Voltaire observed that even the worst abuses can become venerable with age.

Prenuptial agreement. A premarital contract describing how a couple will divide their assets if they ever divorce. Not made at arm's length.

Punitive damages. Damages awarded by a jury to punish a defendant for such outrageous wrongdoing as fraud, recklessness, or being a large corporation.

Quasi. 1. First name of the bellringer of Notre Dame. 2. (Pronounced *kwāzy.*) How you already feel after only two weeks of law school.

Real parties in interest. Often, the lawyers. The clients exist just so somebody's name can appear on the pleadings.

Reasonable person. A hypothetical person who exercises those qualities of prudence, attention, knowledge, intelligence, and judgment that society expects. A truly hypothetical person.

Recidivist. A habitual offender. A person who hasn't learned how to be a productive member of society, even though we locked him in a cell with murderers, thieves, and drug dealers, and taught him such marketable skills as how to clean the prison yard of cigarette butts. Some people just refuse to be helped.

Reductio ad absurdum. Latin for "To reduce to the absurd." When applied to the legal system, a fairly short leap.

Rent-a-judge. Process in which parties rent a retired judge to decide their case. Useful for parties who can't afford to buy a judge of their own.

Repossession. An informal way to satisfy a debt. *E.g.,* if you fail to pay your exorcist, he could have you repossessed.

Respondeat superior. The superior response that you *should* have made to opposing counsel's argument, and that you have brilliantly made a thousand times as you have lain awake every night since then.

Restatement. An effort by the American Law Institute to present a clear and orderly statement of the law. Naturally, it is vehemently opposed by law professors.

Rule of "mereness." A principle that, in legal writing, whatever follows the word "mere" is not so mere. *Cf.* Rule of "clearly."

Scintilla of evidence. Something opponents never have.

Seal. A waxy way of saying "Cross my heart and hope to die," which lawyers can't say because of an anatomical deficiency. In more flexible jurisdictions, a wax sea lion will suffice.

Securities. An oxymoron. Incidentally, why does Chicago, and not New York, have the Bulls and the Bears? (For that matter, why does Utah have the Jazz and New Orleans the Saints?)

Senile dementia. A condition that actually is not so bad. For example, consider all the new friends you get to meet every day. Also, you get to hide your own Easter eggs.

Slander. An oral defamation. If you have to pay damages for slander ruining a law professor's reputation, you'll get change back from your dollar.

Slippery slope. A famous geographical location, not far from the floodgates, where your opponent's argument will always lead.

Stare decisis. Latin for "We stand by our past mistakes." Seventy percent of all legal reasoning is the logical fallacy of appeal to authority. The other forty percent is simply mathematical error.

Statute of frauds. A requirement that certain contracts have a writing. The law could require a writing for large contracts, but that would make too much sense. Instead, certain categories of contracts require a writing. So a contract to guarantee another's five-dollar debt requires a writing, whereas a $12 billion service contract can be oral. Go figure.

Statute of limitations. Rest for the wicked.

Sua sponte. Green Italian ice cream.

Tenure. System under which university professors cannot be fired without adequate cause. Adequate cause does not include either dreadful teaching or the refusal to publish, since these are only secondary to a professor's collegial role. It does include an unexcused absence from the daily bridge game in the faculty lounge.

Traps for the unwary. Scattered throughout the law, these guarantee that only stupid people go to jail. Now if someone could invent a trap for the wary, *that* would be something.

True facts. In litigation, regrettably, not a redundant phrase.

Ultrahazardous activity. Admitting that you are a conservative in a law class. The others will conclude that you are so narrow-minded you can see through a keyhole with both eyes.

Unconscionable contract. A contract that is so unreasonable as to be unenforceable. The test is whether the contract is so unfair that it is impossible to state it to a person of common sense without producing an exclamation at the inequality of it.[65] This is a variation of Justice Stewart's definition of pornography: "I know it when I swear at it."

Unities. The common law requires five unities to create a tenancy by the entirety: the unities of interest, possession, time, title, and person. These five unities, plus the unity of money, are also required to participate in an Erhard Sensitivity Training seminar.

Unjust enrichment. *See* Hourly billing rates.

Unreasonable restraint of trade. In the eyes of the law and economics people, any law.

Vagrancy. A class of offenses that includes idleness, being without meaningful employment, wandering without any purpose or object, and being a "wild rogue." Vagrancy laws have been struck down as being void for vagueness. Nobody could tell whether they were intended to include law professors.

Voir dire. The examination of prospective jurors by the attorneys so they can challenge any jurors who exhibit disqualifying characteristics such as bias, a relationship with a party, or common sense.

Workers' compensation acts. Statutes that make employers strictly liable for their employees' injuries occurring in the course of employment. The payment schedules are updated at least once every 200 years; the amount of damages payable upon the death of a top-notch employee is currently $6.73.

Wraparound mortgage. Something to keep you warm when interest rates leave you out in the cold.

Wrongful-death statutes. Statutes that make a defendant liable for causing another's death. Under the common law, if you injured someone, you were liable for damages. However, if the injured person died, you were not liable to pay anything. This rule encouraged people who intended to hurt someone to give it their best shot.

Zone of danger. Zone close to an accident in which a person must be located to recover damages for the negligent infliction of emotional distress. The boundary of the zone is presently the same as the territorial borders of the United States. Any American who sees an accident on the eleven o'clock news and gets dyspepsia now rushes into court and sues for millions.

---

[65] Toker v. Westerman, 274 A.2d 78, 80 (N.J. Super. 1970) (quoting 43 Words and Phrases 143).

A Bibliography of
Humor and the Law

BOOKS

Bill Adler, *Great Lawyer Stories* (1992).

John Anstey, *The Pleader's Guide* (1808).

Edward J. Bander, *Mr. Dooley on the Choice of Law* (1963).

Edward J. Bander, *Mr. Dooley and Mr. Dunne: The Literary Life of a Chicago Catholic* (1981).

Paul Bergman, *Trial Advocacy in a Nutshell* (2d ed. 1989).

L. J. Bigelow, *Bench and Bar: A Complete Digest of the Wit, Humor, Asperities, and Amenities of the Law* (Johnson Reprint Corp. 1970) (1871).

Simon Bond, *Battered Lawyers* (1990).

Charles Bragg, *Charles Bragg on the Law: A Sardonic View of our Fun-Filled Legal System in Action* (1984).

Jess M. Brallier, *Lawyers and Other Reptiles* (1992).

Marshall Brown, *Wit and Humor of Bench and Bar* (1899).

Irving Browne, *Humorous Phases of the Law* (Fred B. Rothman & Co. 1982) (1876).

Jerry Buchmeyer, *et cetera* (1981).

J. P. C., *Poetic Justice* (1947).

Shneor Z. Cheshin, *Tears and Laughter in an Israeli Courtroom* (Channah Kleinerman trans., 1959).

Anne Condon & Tom Condon, *Legal Lunacy* (1992).

Corpus Juris Humorous (John B. McClay & Wendy L. Matthews, eds., 1991).

J. Greenbag Croke, *Lyrics of the Law* (1884).

John Allison Duncan, *The Strangest Cases on Record* (1940).

Gus C. Edwards, *Legal Laughs: A Joke for Every Jury* (1914).

Elliot Egan, *The Lawyer's Guide to Cheating, Stealing and Amassing Obscene Wealth* (1991).

Sam J. Ervin, Jr., *Humor of a Country Lawyer* (1983).

Eugene C. Gerhart, *Quote It! Memorable Legal Quotations; Data, Epigrams, Wit, and Wisdom from Legal and Literary Sources* (1969).

Eugene C. Gerhart, *Quote It II: A Dictionary of Memorable Legal Quotations* (1988).

Milton D. Green, *It's Legal to Laugh* (1984).

Cameron Harvey, *Legal Wit and Whimsy: An Anthology of Humor* (1988).

Peter Hay, *The Book of Legal Anecdotes* (1989).

Franklin Fiske Heard, *Curiosities of the Law Reporters* (2d ed. 1881).

Franklin Fiske Heard, *Oddities of the Law* (Fred B. Rothman & Co. 1983) (1885).

Kenney F. Hegland, *Introduction to the Study and Practice of Law in a Nutshell* (1983).

A. P. Herbert, *Misleading Cases in the Common Law* (1930).

A. P. Herbert, *Still More Misleading Cases* (1933).

A. P. Herbert, *Uncommon Law* (1936).

A. P. Herbert, *Odd's Last Case* (1952).

A. P. Herbert, *More Uncommon Law* (1982).

K. R. Hobbie, *World's Wackiest Lawsuits* (1992).

Samuel A. Howard, *JurisIMprudence = Corpus Juris Ridiculorum* (1976).

Dick Hyman, *It's Still the Law* (1961).

Dick Hyman, *The Columbus Chicken Statute and More Bonehead Legislation* (1985).

Rodney R. Jones, Charles Sevilla & Gerald F. Uelmen, *Disorderly Conduct* (1987).

Rodney R. Jones & Gerald F. Uelmen, *Supreme Folly* (1990).

George Joseph, *Wigs and Weepers* (1980).

The Judicial Humorist: Collection of Judicial Opinions and Other Frivolities (William L. Prosser ed., 1952).

Juris-Jocular: An Anthology of Modern American Legal Humor (Ronald L. Brown ed., 1988).

Arnold B. Kanter, *The Secret Memoranda of Stanley J. Fairweather* (1981).

Arnold B. Kanter, *Advanced Law Firm Mismanagement* (1993).

Bruce Littlejohn, *Laugh with the Judge: Humorous Anecdotes for a Career on the Bench* (1974).

John G. May, Jr., *The Lighter Side of Law* (1956).

The Oxford Book of Legal Anecdotes (Michael Gilbert ed., 1986).

Robert Wayne Pelton, *Looney Laws That You Never Knew You Were Breaking* (1990).

Robert Wayne Pelton, *Laughable Laws and Courtroom Capers* (1993).

Edward Phillips, *The World's Best Lawyer Jokes* (1989).

Alfred Laurence Polak, *More Legal Fictions: A Series of Cases from Shakespeare* (1946).

Michael Rafferty, *Skid Marks* (1989).

Denys Roberts, *How to Dispense with Lawyers* (1964).

Jonathan Roth & Andrew Roth, *Poetic Justice* (1988).

Jeff Rowan, *500 Great Lawyer Jokes* (1992).

Don Sandburg, *The Legal Guide to Mother Goose* (1978).

Charles M. Sevilla, *Disorder in the Court* (1992).

Harry T. Shafer & Angie Papadakis, *The Howls of Justice* (1988).

Peter F. Sloss, *Alice's Adventures in Jurisprudencia* (1982).

Aron Steuer, *Aesop in the Courts* (1971).

Aron Steuer, *Aesop in the Courts, 2* (1981).

Bob Terrell & Marcellus Buchanan, *Disorder in the Court!* (1984).

Ralph Warner & Toni Ihara, *29 Reasons Not to Go to Law School* (1982).

D. Robert White, *The Official Lawyer's Handbook* (1983).

D. Robert White, *White's Law Dictionary* (1985).

Daniel R. White, *Trials & Tribulations: Appealing Legal Humor* (1989).

Daniel R. White, *Still the Official Lawyer's Handbook* (1991).

John Willock, *Legal Facetiae: Satirical and Humorous* (1887).

Wit and Humor of the American Bar (1905).

Irving Younger, *Imaginary Judicial Opinions* (1989).

ARTICLES

Advertising

W. J. Bolt, *It Pays to Advertise*, 122 Just. of the Peace 821 (1958).

Marianne M. Jennings, *I Can Settle that Case in 90 Days or It's Free*, Ariz. Att'y, Jan. 1993, at 62.

Antitrust

Joseph Sedgwick, *Luncheon Address*, 32 A.B.A. Antitrust L.J. 149 (1966).

Campaign Finance

York Moody Faulkner, *A Negative Incentive Proposal for Campaign Finance Reform: A Lesson from Nottingham*, 1992 B.Y.U. L. Rev. 493.

City Government

J.E.S., *Church Parade*, 121 Just. of the Peace 816 (1957).

Civil Procedure

Robert S. Ryan, *Dajongi Experience: A Comparative Study in Federal Jurisdiction*, 18 Stan. L. Rev. 451 (1966).

Commercial Law

Marianne Moody Jennings, *I Want to Know What Bearer Paper Is and I Want to Meet a Holder in Due Course*, 1992 B.Y.U. L. Rev. 385.

Marianne M. Jennings, *Does Secured Transaction Mean I Have a Lien? Thoughts on Chattel Mortgages (What?) and Other Complexities of Article IX*, 17 Nova L. Rev. 689 (1993).

Common Law

John J. Flynn, *Further Aside, A Comment on "The Common Law Origins of the Infield Fly Rule"*, 4 J. Contemp. L. 233 (1978).

John E. Simonett, *The Common Law of Morrison County*, 49 A.B.A. J. 263 (1963).

Aside, *The Common Law Origins of the Infield Fly Rule*, 123 U. Pa. L. Rev. 1474 (1975).

Computers

Alan Patrick Herbert, *Reign of Error*, 50 Chi. B. Rec. 481 (1969).

Contracts

Douglass G. Boshkoff, *Selected Poems on the Law of Contracts*, 66 N.Y.U. L. Rev. 1533 (1991).

Brainerd Currie, *Aberlone, Rose of*, 59 Case & Com., July–Aug. 1954, at 14.

James D. Gordon III, *A Dialogue About the Doctrine of Consideration*, 75 Cornell L. Rev. 987 (1990).

James D. Gordon III, *Consideration and the Commercial-Gift Dichotomy*, 44 Vand. L. Rev. 283 (1991).

David Eccles Hardy, *Great Cases in Utopian Law*, 6 J. Contemp. L. 227 (1979).

Maurice H. Merrill, *Law's Dislike for Self-appointed Judges*, 10 Okla. L. Rev. 48 (1957).

Special Feature, *We Stoop to Comment—367 F. Supp. 373 (E.D. Pa. 1973)*, 12 Duq. L. Rev. 717 (1974).

Constitutional Law

Boris Bittker, *The Bicentennial of the Jurisprudence of Original Intent*, 77 Cal. L. Rev. 235 (1989).

William Blodgett, *Just You Wait, Harry Blackmun*, 3 Const. Commentary 3 (1986).

David P. Bryden, *A Right to Pastimes?*, 7 Const. Commentary 1 (1990).

David P. Bryden & Daniel A. Farber, *Three Theorems on Judicial Review*, 2 Const. Commentary 5 (1985).

Art Buchwald, *A Buchwald Civil Liberties Sampler*, 5 Civ. Lib. Rev., Jan.–Feb. 1978, at 28.

But cf., Miles v. Augusta, 2 Const. Commentary 1 (1985).

Daniel A. Farber, *"Terminator 2½": The Constitution in an Alternative World*, 9 Const. Commentary 59 (1992).

Richard H. Field, *Frankfurter, J., Concurring . . .*, 71 Harv. L. Rev. 77 (1957).

Dale Gibson, *Not-so-white, the Ten Dwarfs, and the Nine Wise Ones: A Constitutional Fairy-tale*, 18 Manitoba L. J. 1 (1989).

James D. Gordon III, *Free Exercise on the Mountaintop*, 79 Cal. L. Rev. 91 (1991).

James D. Gordon III, *An Unofficial Guide to the Bill of Rights*, 1992 B.Y.U. L. Rev. 371.

Alex Kozinski, *Introduction: Of Profligacy, Piracy, and Private Property*, 13 Harv. J.L. & Pub. Pol'y 17 (1990).

Wayne R. LaFave, *A Fourth Amendment Fantasy: The Last (Heretofore*

Unpublished) Search and Seizure Decision of the Burger Court, 1986 U. Ill. L. Rev. 669.

Douglas O. Linder, *The Two Hundredth Reunion of Delegates to the Constitutional Convention (or, "All Things Considered, We'd Really Rather Be in Philadelphia")*, 1985 Ariz. St. L.J. 823 (1985).

Norman Redlich, *Supreme Court—1833 Term, Foreword: The Constitution—"A Rule for the Government of Courts, as Well as of the Legislature"*, 40 N.Y.U. L. Rev. 1 (1965).

Norman Redlich, *Black-Harlan Dialogue on Due Process and Equal Protection: Overheard in Heaven and Dedicated to Robert B. McKay*, 50 N.Y.U. L. Rev. 20 (1975).

Rodney A. Smolla, *The Supreme Court and the Temple of Doom: A Short Story*, 2 Const. Commentary 41 (1985).

Copyright

Robert F. Balding, *A Socratic Approach to Understanding the Limits (if Any) of Software Copyright Protection*, 28 Jurimetrics J. 153 (1988).

Corporations

Marianne M. Jennings, *Why Corporate Boards Don't Work*, 12 J.L. & Com. 85 (1992).

Criminal Law

William W. Bedsworth, *If You Have No Relative, One Will be Appointed for You Free of Charge: A Brief History of the California Public Relative's Office*, 55 Cal. St. B.J. 323 (1980).

Paul Butters, *The Third Man*, 121 Just. of the Peace 808 (1957).

Paul Butters, *The Mills of God*, 122 Just. of the Peace 824 (1958).

Jesse I. Etelson, *State v. Raskolnikov*, 42 N.Y.U. L. Rev. 2 2 3 (1967).

Kenneth L. Lasson, *To Kill a Mockingbird: Stare Decisis and M'Naghten in Maryland*, 26 Md. L. Rev. 143 (1966).

Kenneth L. Lasson, *Rummel v. Estelle: Mockingbirds Among the Brethren*, 18 Am. Crim. L. Rev. 441 (1981).

John O. Levinson, *Of Game Plans, Powers, and Prerogatives*, 59 A.B.A. J. 373 (1973).

Peter Lushing, *The Exclusionary Rule: A Disputation*, 7 Cardozo L. Rev. 713 (1986).

Maurice H. Merrill, *The Prophet's Mistake*, 11 Okla. L. Rev. 166 (1958).

J. Bennett Miller, *The Trial of Malcolm Gillespie or the Life and Times of an Excise Man*, 1967 Jurid. Rev. 225 (1967).

A.L.P., *Vagaries of the Wayward*, 121 Just. of the Peace 385 (1957).

Richard A. Scarnati, *The Discovery of Hell by a Prison Psychiatrist: A Tragic Satire on the Prison System*, 11 J. Psychiatry & L. 75 (1983).

A Scottish Newsletter, 1962 Crim. L. Rev. 745.

Robert Traver, *The Violator*, 65 Mich. B.J. 428 (1986).

Molly Whittington-Egan, *Letting the Side Down*, 11 Litig., Summer 1985, at 42.

Debtor-Creditor Law

Allan Axelrod, *Was* Shylock v. Antonio *Properly Decided?*, 39 Rutgers L. Rev. 143 (1986).

Environmental Law

James L. Huffman, *Chicken Law in an Eggshell: Part III—A Dissenting Note*, 16 Envtl. L. 761 (1986).

Ethics

Arthur Garwin, *When on Mars*, 17 Nova L. Rev. 941 (1993).

Louis S. Goldberg, *Dialogues on the Lawyer-CPA*, 7 Law Off. Econ. & Mgmt. 265 (1966).

Family Law

James Tillotson Hyde, *His First Case*, 121 Just. of the Peace 812 (1957).

Maurice H. Merrill, *Reflections on the Concept of Unilateral Incompatibility*, 11 Okla. L. Rev. 430 (1958).

Albert M. Rosenblatt, *Matrimonial Lawyers*, 60 N.Y. St. B.J., July 1988, at 56.

International Law

Anthony D'Amato, *It's a Bird, It's a Plane, It's Jus Cogens!*, Conn. J. Int'l L. 1 (1990).

Judicial Administration

Joseph W. Bellacosa, *The Tale of ORCA's Child*, 59 N.Y. St. B.J., Nov. 1987, at 18.

Judicial Opinions

George R. Craig, *Irreverent Verse (Plus Some Irrelevant As Well)*, 7 Duq. L. Rev. 549 (1969).

"Do We Have to Know This for the Exam?", 7 Const. Commentary 223 (1990).

David A. Golden, Comment, *Humor, the Law, and Judge Kozinski's Greatest Hits*, 1992 B.Y.U. L. Rev. 507.

Rodger L. Hochman, *"Good Humor" on the Bench: Just Desserts in a Judicial Diet*, 17 Nova L. Rev. 965 (1993).

Adalberto Jordan, Note, *Imagery, Humor, and the Judicial Opinion*, 41 U. Miami L. Rev. 693 (1987).

James M. Marsh, *Mr. Dooley Discovers a Unanimous Dissent*, 62 Case & Com., Nov.–Dec. 1957, at 8.

Abner Mikva, *Goodbye to Footnotes*, 56 U. Colo. L. Rev. 647 (1985).

Marshall Rudolf, Note, *Judicial Humor: A Laughing Matter?*, 41 Hast. L.J. 175 (1989).

Susan K. Rushing, *Is Judicial Humor Judicious?*, 1 Scribes J. Legal Writing 125 (1990).

Arthur Shacksnovis, *The Opinion in Verse*, 73 S. Afr. L.J. 9 4 (1956).

Bernard Schenkler, *The Duck Maxim*, 140 N.J. Law., May–June 1991, at 44.

George Rose Smith, *A Critique of Judicial Humor*, 43 Ark. L. Rev. 1 (1990).

The Syufy Rosetta Stone, 1992 B.Y.U. L. Rev. 457.

Patric M. Verrone, *The-All-Supreme-Court-Opinion-Baseball-Team*, 17 Nova L. Rev. 933 (1993).

Comment, *Animal Kingdom*, 25 Fordham L. Rev. 577 (1956).

Comment, *The Ridiculous and the Sublime*, 25 Fordham L. Rev. 395 (1956).

Labor Law

George M. Eubanks, *Peaceful Picketing: A Fairy Tale in Three Parts*, 8 J. Pub. L. 308 (1959).

Law Libraries

Edward J. Bander, *Mr. Dooley on Law Librarians*, 89 Libr. J. 575 (1964).

Riley Paul Burton, *As We See Each Other*, 48 Law Libr. J. 364 (1955).

Frances Farmer, *On the Gentle Art of Librating*, 52 Law Libr. J. 127 (1959).

Garrett Hardin, *The Last Canute*, 23 Law Off. Econ. & Mgmt. 2 3 9 (1982–83).

Jim Kelly, *The Meeting o' the AA Double L*, 75 Law Libr. J. 2 8 4 (1982).

David Moore, *The Modern Law Librarian*, 56 Law Libr. J. 452 (1963).

Legal Education

Roger I. Abrams, *Law and the Chicken: An Eggs-agerated Curriculum Proposal*, 17 Nova L. Rev. 771 (1993).

Francis H. Anderson, *Siwash Law School—1980*, 28 Alb. L. Rev. 219 (1964).

Edward J. Bander, . . . *Mr. Dooley on the Case System*, 7 Student Law. J., Dec. 1961, at 19.

Robert D. Bartels, *Report on Faculty Governance*, 42 J. Legal Educ. 299 (1992).

Andrew Beckerman-Rodau, *The Beckerman-Rodau Method: A New Approach to Teaching Law*, 41 J. Legal Educ. 299 (1991).

Paul Bergman, *2010: A Clinical Odyssey*, 1992 B.Y.U. L. Rev. 349.

Burton F. Brody, *A Movie Review*, 26 J. Legal Ed. 605 (1974) (reviewing *The Paper Chase* (20th Century Fox 1973)).

Burton F. Brody & Lawrence P. Tiffany, *Relevance Refined or What the Carrington Report Did Not Dare to Print or What You Always Wanted to Know About Curriculum but Were Too Old to Ask*, 24 J. Legal Ed. 603 (1972).

Anthony D'Amato, *Minutes of the Faculty Meeting*, 1992 B.Y.U. L. Rev. 359.

C. Steven Bradford, *The Gettysburg Address as Written by Law Students Taking an Exam*, 86 Nw. U. L. Rev. 1094 (1992).

Paul Duke, *Rules for Success in Teaching and Examining*, 11 J. Legal Educ. 386 (1959).

James D. Gordon III, *Humor in Legal Education and Scholarship*, 1992 B.Y.U. L. Rev. 313.

James D. Gordon III, *The Trials of Reforming Legal Education*, Chron. Higher Ed., Jan. 22, 1992, at B1.

James D. Gordon III, *How Not to Succeed in Law School*, 100 Yale L.J. 1679 (1991).

Marianne M. Jennings, *CLE for Me*, Ariz. Att'y, Mar. 1992, at 54.

Erik M. Jensen, *A Day in the Life of S. Breckinridge Tushingham*, 69 Denver U. L. Rev. 231 (1992).

Yale Kamisar, *Three Professors Involved in Major Trade: Smith, Leading Antitrust Man, Goes to Yankees*, 11 J. Legal Educ. 549 (1959).

Ali Khan, *Professor Prufrock*, 36 J. Legal Educ. 117 (1986).

Ron Lansing, *Faculty Meetings: "A Quorum Plus Cramshaw"*, 17 Nova L. Rev. 817 (1993).

Paul A. LeBel, *A Guide for the Selection of Faculty Recruiters—". . . or any First Year Course,"* 37 J. Legal Educ. 374 (1987).

Paul A. LeBel, *Diagnosing Posttenure Slump Syndrome: A Guide to the Aging of Law Professors*, 39 J. Legal Educ. 49 (1989).

Paul A. LeBel, *Law Professor Trading Cards—"Has Anyone Got a Monaghan for a Tribe?"*, 38 J. Legal Educ. 365 (1988).

Paul A. LeBel, *There Should Be Some Lively Class Discussions About Trade Once Law Professors Are Carded*, 17 Student Law., Apr. 1989, at 43.

Paul A. LeBel, *Legal Education and the Theater of the Absurd: "Can't Anybody Play This Here Game?"*, 1992 B.Y.U. L. Rev. 413.

Paul A. LeBel & James E. Moleterno, *The Joe Isuzu Dean Search: A Guide to Interpretation*, 39 J. Legal Educ. 265 (1989).

Paul A. LeBel, *Deerly, Departed*, 42 J. Legal Educ. 469 (1992).

Steven Lubet, *A Theory of University Climate*, 39 J. Legal Educ. 51 (1989).

Dan McGurn, *Syllabus*, 17 Nova L. Rev. 893 (1993).

Sandra Craig McKenzie, *Law School: Preparation for Parenthood*, 37 J. Legal Educ. 367 (1987).

Robert W. Miller, *The Weary Dean*, 21 Fed'n Ins. Couns. Q., Spring 1971, at 9.

Ron Ostroff, *The Drudge*, 17 Nova L. Rev. 855 (1993).

Phineas Phogmore, *Aboriginal Legal Education in East Africa*, 14 J. Legal Educ. 353 (1962).

Professor X [pseud.], *Suicidal Admissions and Grading Policies of Our Law Schools,* 13 Prac. Law., Jan. 1967, at 35.

William L. Prosser, *Lighthouse No Good,* 1 J. Legal Educ. 257 (1948).

William L. Prosser, *A Questionnaire for Questioners,* 10 J. Legal Educ. 494 (1958).

William L. Prosser, *The Decline and Fall of the Institut,* 19 J. Legal Educ. 41 (1966).

Robert E. Rains, *Of Clocks and Things,* 39 J. Legal Educ. 259 (1989).

Marc Rohr, *Socrates' Class: A One-Act Play,* 17 Nova L. Rev. 839 (1993).

Louis B. Schwartz, *How to Pass Law School Examinations,* 11 J. Legal Educ. 223 (1958).

Harold See, *Criteria for the Evaluation of Law School Examination Papers,* 38 J. Legal Educ. 361 (1988).

David L. Shapiro, *After Reading Too Many Tenure Files,* 37 J. Legal Educ. 203 (1987).

Marshall S. Shapo, *Propositions of Opposition: A Guide for Faculty Members Engaged in the Assessment of Prospective and Present Colleagues,* 37 J. Legal Educ. 364 (1987).

Grant M. Sumsion, Comment, *Reflections of a 3L—A Thought Piece,* 1992 B.Y.U. L. Rev. 549.

Oren S. Tasini, *Concise Guide to Surviving the First Year of Law School,* 17 Nova L. Rev. 849 (1993).

D. Robert White, *Getting Into the Right Law School ("My Roommate the Moonie Scored in the 98th Percentile on the LSAT and Got Into Harvard. Why Didn't I?"),* 17 Nova L. Rev. 979 (1993).

Legal Language

Edward J. Bander, *Shakespeare for the Law Student,* 5 Duq. L. Rev. 53 (1966–67).

Murray J. Diamond, *Cinderella: Lawyer's Edition,* 57 Case & Com., July–Aug. 1952, at 34.

Vic Fleming, *Fun with Language,* 21 Ark. Law., July 1987, at 106.

Edward A. Hogan III, *A Law Professor's Version of the Three Bears,* 55 Case & Com., Jan.–Feb. 1950, at 27.

Newman Levy, *If Lawyers Talked Like Lawyers,* 64 Case & Com., Jan.–Feb. 1959, at 3.

Robert Wyness Millar, *The Shade of Sir Edward Coke Reports the Baseball Game Played Between the Law School Faculty of Northwestern*

University and the Law Review Editorial Board on Tuesday, the 9th Day of May, 1939, 54 Nw. U. L. Rev. 153 (1959).

Paul Morris, *Dear Paul: Language Tips Questions and Answers*, 17 Nova L. Rev. 729 (1993).

Paul Morris, *How to Win Friends and Impress Clients With Latin*, 17 Nova L. Rev. 991 (1993).

Gerald F. Uelmen, *Plain Yiddish for Lawyers*, 71 A.B.A. J., June 1985, at 78.

Kenneth H. York, *Jack and the Beanstock . . . As Related by a Lawyer to His Son*, 54 Case & Com., May–June 1949, at 11.

Legal Profession

Bond Almand, *Bar Salad with Bench Dressing*, 7 Ga. St. B.J. 75 (1970).

Louis Auchincloss, *The Senior Partner's Ghosts*, 50 Va. L. Rev. 195 (1964).

J.S. Bainbridge, Jr., *Future Fantasy*, 23 Md. B.J., Nov.–Dec. 1990, at 2.

Edward J. Bander, *A Day in the Life of a Suffolk Alumnus: Class of 2001*, Advoc. (Suffolk U. L. Sch.), 1981, at 31.

William W. Bedsworth, *The Screendoor Repairman and Certified Criminal Law Specialist's Examination*, 53 Cal. St. B.J. 186 (1978).

Neal Boortz, *Open Season on Lawyers*, 17 Nova L. Rev. 985 (1993).

Byrne A. Bowman, *General Practitioner Visits a Law Factory*, 51 A.B.A. J. 134 (1965); 109 Solic. J. 729 (1965).

Jess M. Brallier, *Life, Lawyers, and Book Royalties*, 17 Nova L. Rev. 767 (1993).

Art Buchwald, *The Uptight Society*, 3 Civ. Lib. Rev., Aug.–Sept. 1976, at 65.

Art Buchwald, *Commencement Day Address*, 27 Cath. U. L. Rev. 1 (1977).

Art Buchwald, *Bad Lawyers are Very Good for the U.S. Justice System*, 64 A.B.A. J. 328 (1978).

Art Buchwald, *Welcome to the Good New Times*, 65 A.B.A. J. 1138 (1979).

Aubrey M. Cates, Jr., *Be Kind to Lawyers Week*, 23 Ala. Law. 250 (1962).

Erwin Cherovsky, *The Heavenly City of Lawyers*, 59 N.Y. St. B.J., May 1987, at 49.

Frank M. Coffin, *Gullible's Travails: A Prospective Law Student Visits Brobdingnag, a Professional Corporation*, 34 J. Legal Educ. 1 (1984).

Charles S. Desmond, *May It Please the Committee*, 22 Rec. 438 (1967).

Henry Thomas Dolan, *He Who Is His Own . . .* , 22 Shingle 82 (1959).

William Domnarski, *Trouble in Paradise: Wall Street Lawyers and the Fiction of Louis Auchincloss*, 12 J. Contemp. L. 243 (1987).

Arch E. Ekdale, *A Ladd' an His Lamp*, 3 Law Off. Econ. & Mgmt. 409 (1963).

Robert M. Figg, Jr., *Of Carolina Quiddities, Quillets and Cases*, 18 S.C. L. Rev. 719 (1966).

Glen Freyer, *The Nebbish Letter*, 17 Nova L. Rev. 685 (1993).

L.C. Green, *Forensic Facetiae*, 32 Sask. B. Rev. 173 (1967).

Robert C. Hays, *The Disputed Rainbow*, 32 Cal. St. B.J. 651 (1957).

M. James Houlihan, *Four Ways to Save Lawyers' Fees*, 37 Mich. St. B.J., Oct. 1958, at 38.

How to Become a Jurist, 7 J. Soc'y Pub. Tchrs. L. 129 (1963).

Arnold B. Kanter, *Practicing Mice and Other Amazing Tales*, 8 Barrister, Fall 1981, at 18.

Arnold B. Kanter, *Ugly as SIN*, 17 Nova L. Rev. 763 (1993).

Arnold B. Kanter, *The Best of PALS*, 17 Nova L. Rev. 975 (1993).

Tuli Kupferberg, *An Insulting Look at Lawyers Through the Ages*, 8 Juris Dr., Oct.–Nov. 1978, at 62.

F. Ted Laskin, *Lex-in-the-Box: The Great Leap Forward in Marketing Legal Services*, 55 Cal. St. B.J. 366 (1980).

Mortimer Levitan, *Manners for Lawyers*, 29 Ins. Couns. J. 415 (1962); 36 N.Y. St. B.J. 23 (1964); 35 Wis. B. Bull. 6 (1962).

Jim Lorenz, *Making the World Safe for Lawyers*, 35 NLADA Briefcase 154 (1978).

Robert J. Morris, Comment, *The New (Legal) Devil's Dictionary*, 6 J. Contemp. L. 231 (1979).

Bob W. Murphey, *That's My Opinion . . . I Think*, 49 Neb. L. Rev. 397 (1969).

Don Musser, *Exposition on the Preparation and Use of Expert Testimony—A Satire*, 42 Neb. L. Rev. 396 (1962).

Howard L. Oleck, *The Pompous Professions*, 18 Clev.–Marshall L. Rev. 276 (1969).

Luther Patrick, *Lawyer, Take My Case*, 17 Ala. Law. 392 (1956).

Nicholas Perry, *Old Lag's Law*, 123 Just. of the Peace 36 (1959).

Elton B. Richey, Jr., *The Court Jesters*, 41 Mercer L. Rev. 663 (1990).

Asher Rubin, *The Supreme Moment*, 23 Harv. L. Sch. Bull., Feb. 1972, at 13.

Jerry Schwartz, *Art Buchwald at the Bar*, 4 Civ. Lib. Rev., Jan.–Feb. 1978, at 35.

Ron Suskind, *A Lady Lawyer in Laramie Writes a Landmark Letter*, Wall St. J., September 6, 1990, at 1.

Frank G. Swain, *Therapy of Humor in the Practice of Law*, 50 Law Libr. J. 200 (1957).

Jeff Tolman, *My Malpractice Trial*, 71 A.B.A. J., Aug. 1985, at 70.

Gerald F. Uelmen, *Id.*, 1992 B.Y.U. L. Rev. 335.

Richard W. Wallach, *Let's Have a Little Humor*, 191 N.Y. L.J., Mar. 30, 1984, at 2.

Ralph Warner & Toni Ihara, *Becoming a Partner*, 17 Nova L. Rev. 951 (1993).

Sterry R. Waterman, *Remarks*, 49 B.U. L. Rev. 584 (1969).

D. Robert White, *Recruiting Letters*, 17 Nova L. Rev. 709 (1993).

Margaret D. White, *Soul Searching for Fox Paws*, Ariz. Att'y, Dec. 1992, at 62.

Charles E. Whittaker, *Some Reminiscences*, 43 Neb. L. Rev. 352 (1964).

Legal Scholarship

Arthur D. Austin, *Why Haven't the Crits Deconstructed Footnotes?*, 17 Nova L. Rev. 725 (1993).

Ronald L. Brown, *Rave Reviews: The Top Ten Law Journals of the 1990s*, 12 Legal Reference Services Q. 121 (1992).

Daniel A. Farber, *Gresham's Law of Legal Scholarship*, 3 Const. Commentary 307 (1986).

James D. Gordon III, *Law Review and the Modern Mind*, 33 Ariz. L. Rev. 265 (1991).

Kenney Hegland, *Humor as the Enemy of Death, or Is It "Humor as the Enemy of Depth"?*, 1992 B.Y.U. L. Rev. 375.

Erik M. Jensen, *A Call for a New Buffalo Law Scholarship*, 38 U. Kan. L. Rev. 433 (1990).

Erik M. Jensen, *The Unwritten Article*, 17 Nova L. Rev. 785 (1993).

J. T. Knight, *Humor and the Law*, 1993 Wis. L. Rev. 897.

Paul A. LeBel, *A Revue of Books*, 35 J. Legal Educ. 299 (1985).

John M. Lindsey, *Academic Law Review Writing*, 17 Nova L. Rev. 917 (1993).

William L. Prosser, *Der Gegenverkehr des Wasserniedersinkens in der nordlichen und der sudlichen Hemisphare*, 51 Minn. L. Rev. 899 (1967).

Fred Rodell, *Goodbye to Law Reviews*, 23 Va. L. Rev. 38 (1936).

Fred Rodell, *Goodbye to Law Reviews—Revisited*, 48 Va. L. Rev. 279 (1962).

William R. Slomanson, *Do's and Taboos for Making Law Review: A Law Student's Compass*, 11 Crim. Just. J. 489 (1989).

Carl Tobias, *Elixir for the Elites*, 76 Iowa L. Rev. 353 (1991).

Patric M. Verrone, *Notes and Comments: A Law Review Article*, 17 Nova L. Rev. 733 (1993).

Legal System

Edward J. Bander, *The Dooley Process of Law*, 62 Case & Com., Sept.–Oct. 1957, at 20.

Edward J. Bander, *Mr. Dooley and the Law*, 36 N.Y. St. B.J. 336 (1964).

Edward J. Bander, *Mr. Dooley and the Chicago Bar*, 54 Ill. B.J. 318 (1965).

Dave Barry, *Traffic Infraction, He Wrote*, 17 Nova L. Rev. 665 (1993).

Dave Barry, *Pain and Suffering*, 17 Nova L. Rev. 999 (1993).

Kent M. Bridwell, *The Powdered Wig Conspiracy: A Brief Exposé of Legal Wit and Humor*, 52 L.A. B.J. 614 (1977).

Maxwell Cohen, *A Canadian Looks at American Law and Justice*, 36 B. Examiner 35 (1967).

Frank E. Cooper, *Should Administrative Hearing Procedures be Less Fair Than Criminal Trials?*, 53 A.B.A. J. 237 (1967).

Joseph Eckhaus, Comment, *Unhallowed Loathsome Perceptions*, 22 J. Legal Educ. 89 (1969).

L.C. Green, *The Lighter Side of the Law*, 31 Sask. B. Rev. 162 (1966).

A. Leon Higginbotham, *Luncheon Address*, 37 A.B.A. Antitrust L.J. 748 (1968).

Otto M. Kaus, *Bar Wars*, 53 Cal. St. B.J. 86 (1978).

John A. Kidwell, *The Day the Machine Broke Down*, 69 A.B.A. J. 50 (1983).

Paul A. LeBel, *The Bases Are Loaded and it's Time to Get a Restraining Order: The Confounding Conflation of America's Two National Pastimes*, 17 Nova L. Rev. 813 (1993).

James G. Manning, Jr., *A Phantastic Phantasy*, 63 Case & Com., July–Aug. 1958, at 20.

Brian McKenna, *The Judge and the Common Man*, 32 Mod. L. Rev. 601 (1969).

Robert E. Megarry, *Temptations of the Bench*, 16 Alberta L. Rev. 406 (1978).

David Mellinkoff, *Who Is "John Doe"?*, 12 UCLA L. Rev. 79 (1964).

Maurice H. Merrill, *The Arkansawyer's Lament*, 10 Okla L. Rev. 167 (1957).

Roslyn Moore-Silver, *Laughter Is Legal*, 27 Ariz. Att'y, May 1991, at 15.

W.G. Morrow, *The Last Case*, 16 Alberta L. Rev. 1 (1978).

J. Richard Neville, Comment, *Humorous Anecdotes of the Georgia Judiciary, 1884–1920*, 41 Mercer L. Rev. 655 (1990).

A.L.P., *"These Troublesome Disguises" (A Reminiscence)*, 122 Just. of the Peace 308 (1958).

Barbara Kate Repa, *Legal Lunacy 1986*, 15 Student Law., Dec. 1986, at 22.

Barbara Kate Repa, *True Stories: Legal Lunacies 1987*, 16 Student Law., Dec. 1987, at 29.

Barbara Kate Repa, *Legal Lunacy 1988*, 17 Student Law., Dec. 1988, at 15.

Barbara Kate Repa, *Legal Lunacy 1989*, 18 Student Law., Dec. 1989, at 15.

Barbara Kate Repa, *Legal Lunacy 1990*, 19 Student Law., Dec. 1990, at 27.

Charles Ritchie Russell, *Profile for the Future: Law and Society in the Year 2000*, 52 A.B.A. J. 915 (1966).

Charles M. Sevilla, *Great/Fractured Moments in Courtroom History*, 17 Nova L. Rev. 699 (1993).

Scott M. Solkoff, *If the Law Is a Jealous Mistress, What Ever Happened to Pay Toilets? A Digest of the Legally Profound*, 17 Nova L. Rev. 715 (1993).

Charles Stone, *Voir Dire: Just When You Think You've Heard It All*, 17 Nova L. Rev. 867 (1993).

Moses Torts [pseud.], Comment, *A Twenty-Fifth Annual Special: The Law from Moses Forward*, 25 S.D. L. Rev. 208 (1980).

J. Neville Turner, *Celebrated, Cultivated but Underrated? W.S. Gilbert as a Legal Satirist*, 9 U. Tasmania L. Rev. 117 (1988).

Gerald F. Uelmen, *The Care and Feeding of TV Court Critics*, 17 Nova L. Rev. 825 (1993).

Robert Watts, *An American Counterclaim*, 77 S. Afr. L.J. 240 (1960).

Benjamin Wham, *Judicial Education of Henry Adams—Or Was It Just the Beginning?*, 52 A.B.A. J. 365 (1966).

Bernard Witkin, *120-Proof Program of Unlikely Reforms in the Law*, 56 Law Libr. J. 31 (1963).

Douglas E. Winter, *Down-Time: A Fable*, 13 Litig. Fall 1986, at 48.

Writers of the David Letterman Show, *The Top 10 Ways the Justice System Would Be Different if Bears Sat on Juries*, 17 Nova L. Rev. 997 (1993).

Legal Theory

Daniel H. Benson, *The You Bet Metaphorical Reconstructionist School*, 37 J. Legal Educ. 210 (1987).

Craig Brownlie, *Marxism and Critical Legal Theory: Why Groucho?* 17 Nova L. Rev. 921 (1993).

Anthony D'Amato, *The Ultimate Critical Legal Studies Article: A Fissiparous Analysis*, 37 J. Legal Educ. 369 (1987).

Anthony D'Amato, *As Gregor Samsa Awoke One Morning from Uneasy Dreams He Found Himself Transformed into an Economic Analyst of Law*, 83 Nw. U. L. Rev. 1012 (1989). (*See also Gregor Samsa Replies*, 83 Nw. U. L. Rev. 1022 (1989)).

Richard Delgado & John Kidwell, *Recent Developments in Legal Theory: How to Compare Apples and Oranges*, 7 Const. Commentary 209 (1990).

Daniel A. Farber, *An Economic Analysis of Abortion*, 3 Const. Commentary 1 (1986).

Daniel A. Farber, *The Case Against Brilliance*, 70 Minn. L. Rev. 917 (1986).

Daniel A. Farber, *Brilliance Revisited*, 72 Minn. L. Rev. 367 (1987).

Daniel A. Farber, *Post-Modern Dental Studies*, 4 Const. Commentary 219 (1987).

Daniel A. Farber, *The Deconstructed Grocery List*, 7 Const. Commentary 213 (1990).

Daniel A. Farber, *The Jurisprudential Cab Ride: A Socratic Dialogue*, 1992 B.Y.U. L. Rev. 363.

Kenney Hegland, *Indeterminacy: I Hardly Knew Thee*, 33 Ariz. L. Rev. 509 (1991).

Kenny Hegland & James D. Gordon III, *Deconstruction Letters*, 17 Nova L. Rev. 994 (1993).

Alex Kozinski, *What I Ate for Breakfast and Other Mysteries of Judicial Decisionmaking*, 43 Cons. Fin. L.Q. Rep. 254 (1989).

William L. Prosser, *My Philosophy of Law*, 27 Cornell L.Q. 292 (1942) (book review).

David L. Shapiro, *The Death of the Up-Down Distinction*, 36 Stan. L. Rev. 465 (1985).

Aviam Soifer, *Confronting Deep Strictures: Robinson, Rickey, and Racism*, 6 Cardozo L. Rev. (1985).

William Twining, *The Great Juristic Bazaar*, 14 J. Soc'y Pub. Tchrs. L. 185 (1978).

Adam Winkler & Joshua Davis, *Postmodernism and Dworkin: The View From Half-Court*, 17 Nova L. Rev. 799 (1993).

Legal Writing

W. Duane Benton, Book Review, 86 Yale L.J. 197 (1976) (reviewing *A Uniform System of Citation* (12th ed. 1976)).

Book Review, 68 A.B.A. J. 735 (1982) (reviewing *A Uniform System of Citation* (13th ed. 1981)).

William Brockett, *Battlestar Syntactica: Computer Law for the 1980s*, 54 Cal. St. B.J. 380 (1979).

David P. Bryden, *The Devil's Casebook*, 3 Const. Commentary 313 (1986).

Jim C. Chen, *Something Old, Something New, Something Borrowed, Something Blue*, 58 U. Chi. L. Rev. 1527 (1991) (reviewing *The Bluebook: A Uniform System of Citation* (15th ed. 1991)).

R.B. Craswell, *On Publishing Comic Verse in Law Reviews*, 38 J. Legal Educ. 359 (1988).

James D. Gordon III, *Oh No! A New Bluebook!*, 90 Mich. L. Rev. 1698 (1992) (reviewing *The Bluebook: A Uniform System of Citation* (15th ed. 1991)).

Arnold B. Kanter, *Putting Your Best Footnote Forward*, 9 Barrister, Spring 1982, at 42.

Herma Hill Kay, *In Defense of Footnotes*, 32 Ariz. L. Rev. 41 (1990).

Peter Lushing, Book Review, 67 Colum. L. Rev. 599 (1967) (reviewing *A Uniform System of Citation* (11th ed. 1967)).

Charles R. Maher, *The Infernal Footnote,* 70 A.B.A. J., April 1984, at 92.

Plain Wayne [pseud.], *Gift of an Orange,* 48 Wis. B. Bull., Feb. 1975, at 61.

Antonin Scalia, *Judicial Conference—Federal Circuit,* 128 F.R.D. 452 (1990).

Herbert T. Silsby II, *George H. Smith: Reporter of Decisions Extraordinary,* 64 A.B.A. J. 699 (1978).

William R. Slomanson, Book Review, 39 Okla. L. Rev. 565 (1986) (reviewing *A Uniform System of Citation* (14th ed. 1986)).

Alan Strasser, *Technical Due Process: ?,* 12 Harv. C.R.–C.L. L. Rev. 507 (1977) (reviewing *A Uniform System of Citation* (12th ed. 1976)).

Lindsay T. Thompson, *Homage to Robert Benchley—A Short History of the Footnote,* 45 Wash. St. B. News, April 1991, at 10.

J. Tim Willette, *Memo of Masochism (Reflections in Legal Writing),* 17 Nova L. Rev. 869 (1993).

Aside, *Don't* Cry** Over Filled Milk: The Neglected Footnote Three to Carolene Products***,* 136 U. Pa. L. Rev. 1553 (1988).

Legislation

Jared Tobin Finkelstein, *In re Brett: The Sticky Problem of Statutory Construction,* 42 Fordham L. Rev. 430 (1983).

H. Pomerantz & S. Breslin, *Judicial Humor—Construction of a Statute—Regina v. Ojibway,* 8 Crim. L.Q. 137 (1965).

Philip Schuchman, *In re: Social Science in the Eastern District of Pennsylvania, United States District Court, Middle District, Nusquamia* (*Counsel Have Asked to Remain Anonymous*), 32 U. Pitt. L. Rev. 463 (1971).

Mark J. Zimmermann, *The Prosecutor's Blue Suit,* 88 Case & Com., July–Aug. 1983, at 40.

Note, *Legislative and Judicial Dynamism in Arkansas:* Poisson v. d'Avril, 22 Ark. L. Rev. 724 (1968).

Litigation

William H. Allen & Alex Kozinski, Book Review, 94 Harv. L. Rev. 312 (1980) (reviewing *Rules of the Supreme Court* (1980)).

Art Buchwald, *Inside the Jury Room,* 7 Litig., Fall 1980, at 44.

E. Day Carman, *Another Slant . . . Home Court Advantage*, 52 Cal. St. B.J., Jan.–Feb. 1977, at 32.

Donald J. Evans, *Forgotten Trial Techniques: The Wager of Battle*, 71 A.B.A. J., May 1985, at 66.

Joey Green, *Cliff-hanger Justice* (Part One), Nat'l Lampoon, Aug. 1982, at 14.

Joey Green, *Cliff-hanger Justice* (Part Two), Nat'l Lampoon, Sept. 1982, at 20.

Joey Green, *Cliff-hanger Justice* (Part Three), Nat'l Lampoon, Oct. 1982, at 16.

Alex Kozinski, *The Wrong Stuff*, 1992 B.Y.U. L. Rev. 325.

Charles E. Moylan, Jr., *Res Gestae, or Why Is That Event Speaking and What Is It Doing in This Courtroom?*, 63 A.B.A. J. 968 (1977).

Milt Policzer, *Winning Without Trial*, 14 Litig., Winter 1988, at 43.

Antonin Scalia, *Judicial Proceedings—D.C. Circuit*, 124 F.R.D. 283 (1988).

Jacob A. Stein, *Believe Me It Happened. I Was There*, 15 Litig., Winter 1989, at 42.

Military Law

Charles A. White, Jr., *Judge Advocate General—1983*, 46 Judge Advoc. J. Bull., Oct. 1974, at 41.

Miscellaneous

Albert P. Blaustein, *Space Lawyer*, 61 Case & Com., Mar.–Apr. 1956, at 16.

James D. Peden *Assault and Flattery: A Texas Legend*, 17 Nova L. Rev. 955 (1993).

The Green Bag, v. 1–15 (1889–1903).

Personalities

Edward J. Bander, *Homespun Humor*, 10 Vill. L. Rev. 92, 299, 503 (1964–65).

James D. Gordon III, *Cardozo's Baseball Card*, 44 Stan. L. Rev. 899 (1992) (reviewing Richard A. Posner, *Cardozo: A Study in Reputation* (1990)).

Winfield B. Hale, *John S. Wilkes: Judicial Humorist*, 23 Tenn. L. Rev. 255 (1954).

Walter B. Jones, *Anecdotes About Governor Thomas G. Jones of Alabama*, 17 Ala. Law. 288 (1956).

Alex Kozinski, *My Pizza with Ninó*, 12 Cardozo L. Rev. 1583 (1991).

Barry G. Silverman, *Annual Dinner Pays Witty Tribute to Departing Dean*, 13 ASU L. Forum (Arizona State University College of Law), Spring 1990, at 28.

David Cohn, *Snakes, Bananas and Buried Treasure: The Case for Practical Jokes*, 17 Nova L. Rev. 883 (1993).

Property

Wilmore Brown, *Comedy of the Court*, 32 Ohio B. 1055 (1959).

Paul T.W. Butters, *Third Time Unlucky*, 120 Just. of the Peace 801 (1956).

Kenneth Lasson, *Mad Dogs and Englishmen:* Pierson v. Post [*A Ditty Dedicated to Freshman Law Students, Confused on the Merits*], 17 Nova L. Rev. 857 (1993).

Barton Leach, *The Return of Legal Poets*, 30 Harv. L. Rec., Mar. 3, 1960, at 12.

Frederick M. Nicholas et al., *Perils of Paul or What to Do Until the Lawyer Comes*, 2 J. Beverly Hills B. Ass'n, Nov. 1968, at 30.

A.L.P., *Ill Met By Moonlight*, 122 Just. of the Peace 337 (1958).

William L. Prosser, *Needlemann on Mortgages*, 9 J. Legal Educ. 489 (1957).

Remedies

R.B. Craswell, *Ballade of Distributional Considerations*, 39 J. Legal Educ. 54 (1989).

Securities Regulation

James D. Gordon III, *Interplanetary Intelligence About Promissory Notes as Securities*, 69 Tex. L. Rev. 383 (1990).

Marianne M. Jennings, *Let's Have Liability, More Liability, and No Case Law: Due Diligence, 10Qs, 10Ks, and $10Ms (as in Average Verdict)*, 22 Sw. U. L. Rev. 373 (1993).

Supreme Court

Marianne M. Jennings, *Golf and the Supreme Court*, Ariz. Att'y, July 1992, at 46.

Taxation

Boris I. Bittker, *The Case of the Fictitious Taxpayer: The Federal Taxpayer's Suit Twenty Years After* Flast v. Cohen, 36 U. Chi. L. Rev. 364 (1969).

Boris I. Bittker, *Tax Shelters for the Poor?*, 51 Taxes 68 (1973).

Walter J. Blum, *Nonagression Revisited in a Nutshell: A Satirical View of Mr. Wormser's Plea*, 20 J. Tax'n 186 (1964).

Walter J. Blum, *Anthropological Notes on Federal Tax Men*, 46 Taxes 499 (1968).

Walter J. Blum, *Tax Trends and Tendencies Today*, 52 Taxes 466 (1974).

Walter J. Blum & Willard H. Pedrick, *Estate and Gift Taxation: A Preliminary Report on an Underdeveloped Project of the American Institute of Legal Jurimetrics*, 43 Taxes 636 (1965).

Walter J. Blum & Willard H. Pedrick, *Estate and Gift Tax Retackled: A Progress Report on the AILJ*, 44 Taxes 737 (1966).

Walter J. Blum & Willard H. Pedrick, *Blood, Sweat and Tiers: The Last of the AILJ*, 47 Taxes 76 (1969).

Walter J. Blum & Willard H. Pedrick, *The Reform School Approach to Estate and Gift Tax Revision*, 51 Taxes 81 (1973).

Edwin S. Cohen, *Ode to the Code, or Four Hundred Fights at the Forum, or What Do You Think Your Spouse Has Been Doing on the First Monday Night in the Month?*, 36 Tax Law., 760 (1983).

Nina J. Crimm, *True Confessions to a Collared Tax Professor*, 38 J. Legal Educ. 363 (1988).

Kenneth Culp Davis, *The Case of the Real Taxpayer: A Reply to Professor Bittker*, 36 U. Chi. L. Rev. 375 (1968).

Peter L. Faber, *Complexity in the Tax Laws and Tax Reform: A Modern Fable*, 4 J. Corp. Tax'n 42 (1977).

Erik M. Jensen, *Food for Thought and Thoughts About Food: Can Meals and Lodging Provided to Domestic Servants Be for the Convenience of the Employer?*, 75 Ind. L.J. 639 (1990).

Erik M. Jensen, *The Heroic Nature of Tax Lawyers*, 140 U. Pa. L. Rev. 367 (1991) (reviewing John Grisham, *The Firm* (1991)).

Erik M. Jensen, *A Monologue on the Taxation of Business Gifts*, 1992 B.Y.U. L. Rev. 397.

Marjorie E. Kornhauser, *The Way of the Code*, 39 J. Legal Educ. 47 (1989).

Converse Murdoch & Roy A. Wentz, *The Kidnap and Sky-Jack Victims' Tax Reform Act of 1971*, 25 Tax Law. 141 (1971).

Gail Levin Richmond & Carol A. Roehrenbeck, *From Tedious to Trendy: A Tax Teacher's Triumph*, 17 Nova L. Rev. 739 (1993).

Walter N. Trenerry, *Literary Pilgrim's Progress Along Section 501(c)(3)*, 51 A.B.A. J. 252 (1965).

Torts

Randy T. Austin, *Better Off with the Reasonable Man Dead, or the Reasonable Man Did the Darndest Things*, 1992 B.Y.U. L. Rev. 479.

Robert S. Brumbaugh, *Justice and Jurisprudence: A Socratic Dialogue on Martyn v. Dolin*, 35 Conn. B.J. 127 (1961).

Robert S. Brumbaugh, *Protection from One's Self: A Socratic Dialogue on Maycock v. Martin*, 42 Conn. B.J. 465 (1968).

David Gray Carlson, Cartoon, *Tales of the Unforseen*, 27 Hast. L.J. 776 (1976).

Ray Jay Davis, *Book Review*, 24 J. Legal Educ. 497 (1972) (reviewing Page Keeton & Robert E. Keeton, *Cases and Materials on the Law of Torts* (1971)).

Ian Frazier, *Coyote v. Acme*, The New Yorker, Feb. 26, 1990, at 42.

Robert C. Hays, *Law Not Reasonable*, 31 Cal. St. B.J. 504 (1956).

Joseph W. Little, *Justice for Luigi*, 7 J. Legal Prof. 153 (1982).

John T. Lynch, *Investigators Uncork Good Ones in an Area Where Humor is Rare*, 37 Mich. St. B.J., Oct. 1958, at 18.

Michael L. Richmond, *The Annotated Cordas*, 17 Nova L. Rev. 899 (1993).

Tillotson [pseud.], *Publishing a Libel*, 122 Just. of the Peace (1958).

Comment, *Cradle to Grave*, 24 Fordham L. Rev. 723 (1955–56).

Wills and Estates

Walter Blum, *Is Estate Planning Still with It?*, 49 Taxes 659 (1971).

Jerry Buchmeyer, *The Oberweiss Will*, 45 Tex. B.J. 145 (1982).

Oscar Cuesta, *A Last Will and Testament*, 62 Case & Com., Nov.–Dec. 1957, at 38.

John Wiley Gould, Recent Case, 47 Or. L. Rev. 88 (1967).

Jacob Fisher, *Human Drama in Death and Taxes*, 110 Tr. & Est. 727 (1971).

Elmer M. Million, *Humor in or of Wills*, 11 Vand. L. Rev. 737 (1958).

Elmer M. Million, *Wills: Witty, Witless, and Wicked*, 7 Wayne L. Rev. 335 (1960).

Max C. Peterson, *Aunt Phoebe's Estate Plan: or "Beware the Joint Tenancy"*, 31 Res Gestae 269 (1987).

Stanley Rubenstein, *Pleasure of Making a Will*, 114 Law J. 752 (1964).

L.A. Sheridan, *Power to Appoint for a Non-charitable Purpose: A Duologue or Endacott's Ghost*, 13 DePaul L. Rev. 210 (1963).

Index